GOD
SECRETS

a life filled with

words of knowledge

SHAWN BOLZ
FOREWORD BY GRAHAM COOKE

Published by ICreate Productions,
PO Box 50219, Studio City, CA 91614
www.bolzministries.com

To contact the author about speaking at your conference or church, please go
to www.bolzministries.com

Hardcover ISBN 978-1-942306-93-1
Paperback ISBN 978-1-942306-98-6
eISBN 978-1-947165-00-7

Printed in the United States of America.

Scripture indicates that God shares His secrets with His servants the prophets. It is also not a coincidence that the father of faith, Abraham, also called a friend of God, is the first person in the Bible referred to as a prophet. What do I derive from that? God loves friendship! He loves to share His secret "knowings" with people of genuine faith and relational intimacy. I have known Shawn Bolz and watched his growth in character and gifting for twenty-five years, and I have observed firsthand his walk of love for God and His people. It is my delight and honor to commend to you the message and ministry of Shawn Bolz for such a time as this.

JAMES W. GOLL
Founder, God Encounters Ministries International
Speaker and bestselling author
www.godencounters.com

Shawn Bolz has been used by the Lord effectively in the charisms of the Spirit, and especially in what Scripture refers to as "a word of knowledge." While scholars debate the exact interpretation of that gift, the Pentecostal and charismatic traditions are rooted in a biblical awareness and richly textured experience of God revealing the secrets of hearts by way of this manifestation of the Holy Spirit. Enjoy what Shawn has collected here for you to consider, as he is no stranger to what we have known in terms of how the word of knowledge is expressed.

DR. MARK J. CHIRONNA
Church On The Living Edge, Mark Chironna Ministries, The Issachar Initiative
www.markchironna.com

At a time when it's more important than ever to hear God clearly, along comes *God Secrets*, removing performance-based ministry and inviting us into relational communication with God. Shawn Bolz makes hearing God understandable and prophetic ministry relatable. In so doing, he gives us the tools to make a heart connection with God and others. I highly recommend this book!

BOB HAZLETT
Author of *The Roar: God's Sound in a Raging World*
www.bobhazlett.org

I have known Shawn Bolz for many years and have always found him to be authentic and fully committed to Christ and His kingdom. He is truly a friend of God. When he began having extraordinary and specific words of knowledge, I was blown away. I loved witnessing God reveal secrets to him. He humbly waited on God in a meeting and presented the words he believed the Lord had given him. You could hear a pin drop as the crowds waited in holy anticipation for what God would speak. When the words were delivered, shock and awe filled the atmosphere. The words were so specific and personal that everyone knew he could not have received the insight from a natural source—God was in their midst. Faith would rise in the room and people would be captured by the Lord's glorious presence. As I read *God Secrets*, I was blessed beyond measure. Why? Because Shawn openly and candidly shares what God has taught him. I believe you will gain valuable insights into the heart of God and the operations of the prophetic, but you will also receive powerful invitation and impartation as you read. God is raising up an army of friends. *God Secrets* will help you journey into this holy friendship with God.

PATRICIA KING
Founder, Patricia King Ministries, Women in Ministry Network
www.patriciaking.com

Shawn Bolz is the tip of the spear of true revelatory prophecy. There are many prophecies but few fathers in the prophetic. Shawn is that father and that close brother who everyone wishes they knew. From A to Z, this book completely and thoroughly answers the question, "Wow, Shawn, how do you do that?". Prophets today do great when they prophesy the big picture, how things are versus how things appear. They prophesy over nations and around the earth. Shawn? He's different. He prophesies into people's hearts saved or unsaved! That puts him in a whole different sphere—a sphere and anointing, that, frankly, finally gets the job done. It gets people saved and lives changed. Run, don't walk, to get this book, and please, get a second one for a friend!

STEVE SHULTZ
Founder, The Elijah List
www.elijahlist.com

The Word of God declares that God will not do anything without revealing His secret plans to His friends the prophets. To be a friend of God one must spend time developing an intimate relationship of trust with the Holy Spirit to know His voice, ways, manners and moods. Shawn Bolz's book *God Secrets* is profound in its span and reach as a training guide. *God Secrets* will take the reader behind the veil to help you develop the gift of the word of knowledge. God wants to share His secrets with His beloved bride but we must study the Word of God and the gifts of the Spirit to show ourselves worthy of being approved. This wonderful book will empower you to excel while ministering under the anointing of God because you will begin to recognize, know and understand the heart of the Father.

DR. BARBIE L. BREATHITT
Prophetic Dream Life Coach, Breath of the Spirit Ministries Inc.
www.BarbieBreathitt.com, www.MyOnar.com, Dream Interpretation

In this hour, I'm not sure there is a more important topic for us as believers than how to hear God's voice for ourselves and for others. God is speaking and our great privilege is to hear Him and speak for Him. The profound impact Shawn Bolz is having is not simply due to his gifting. In addition to operating in the gift of word of knowledge at a high level, he has a genuine heart to equip and empower others to do the same. Shawn is making the prophetic accessible to everyone as God intended it to be. I appreciate that Shawn is calling us to lean into what God is saying and that he is using his gift to equip us to hear the voice of God. It has impacted my life and our local community in a powerful way.

BANNING LIEBSCHER
Jesus Culture Founder
jesusculture.com

God Secrets is an astonishing book that equips us to operate in prophetic ministry at a much higher level than we've known. Shawn Bolz's incredible prophetic gift is an invitation to us all to crank up the risk and move into greater accuracy of prophetic ministry by focusing on the Father's love. Don't miss out!

ROBBY DAWKINS
Author and international conference speaker on how to do what Jesus did
robbydawkins.com

Words of knowledge are our Father's way of capturing people's attention. Believers who hear the Father's heart through words of knowledge have incredible doors of opportunity to share the love of Jesus in ordinary environments! Shawn Bolz is an amazing man of God with a powerful gift of the prophetic on his life. He is an incredible teacher and also a personal friend. What I truly love about Shawn is that his teachings are centered on our identity as sons and daughters. Through Shawn's teachings, people are being activated to live fully dependent on the Holy Spirit.

TODD WHITE
www.lifestylechristianity.com

Over the years I have noticed that the prophetic movement can be quite a contentious issue for the body of Christ. I believe that can truly change by the strengthening of one key component: humility. Humility is the foundation of the Kingdom as revealed by Jesus Christ: the unfathomable act of God becoming man. Shawn Bolz displays a level of humility with his prophetic gift in a way I have not seen in any other. In his new book, *God Secrets*, Shawn shares the riches of the secrets that God has revealed to him, while at the same time encouraging the reader to step out and do the same. This book is dripping with humility and is a massive faith-building gift to the body. I would honestly recommend it to anyone and everyone who's hungry for this stuff.

BRIAN "HEAD" WELCH
Co-founder of KoRn
Author, *Save Me from Myself, Stronger* and *With My Eyes Wide Open*
www.brianheadwelch.net

Shawn writes this special book, *God Secrets*, with such a humble heart. His goal is to use his journey, even his mistakes, to help you be bolder and to take risks to share God's love. Shawn's life is a powerful example to us all. He shines for Jesus. God uses words of knowledge and prophesy to connect with people and to minister His deep love and mercy. It is not about you; it is all about Him. I pray that this book will inspire you to step out for God and let Him use you to transform lives.

HEIDI G. BAKER PHD
Co-founder and CEO, Iris Global
www.irisglobal.org

In my almost 40 years of being around the prophetic ministry, Shawn Bolz has one of the most amazing operations of the word of knowledge that I have ever witnessed. In his book *God Secrets*, Shawn shares powerful personal stories of how the word of knowledge is used to connect people to the heart of the Father and to His love and personal nature. But I love that he goes beyond this and encourages the reader that the gift of the Holy Spirit is reproducible in the life of every believer. As you read, you will be challenged to take risks in stepping out of your spiritual comfort zone to rise to the call to make God real everywhere you go! Blessings,

JANE HAMON
christianinternational.com

I have known Shawn for 10 years now and have had the privilege of being in the room on many occasions as he has stepped out in faith with incredible words of knowledge. His gift is truly breathtaking, but his love for God and for people is what has impressed me most about Shawn over the years. I know this book on words of knowledge will compel you to love people where they are at, while encouraging you to risk more and deepen your own personal relationship with God.

BRYAN TORWALT
Jesus Culture
jesusculture.com

Since I was 16 years old, I have been amazed by and deeply impacted by prophetic words and words of knowledge. Nearly every significant aspect of my life—my career, my husband, my home, my child, and much more—was prophesied before it came into physical manifestation. This is why I'm so excited that Shawn Bolz has written *God Secrets*, and is sharing his profound prophetic gift and insights with the world. In this book, Shawn is letting people in on how the incredibly supernatural, yet powerfully personal, gifts of prophecy and words of knowledge work—a true asset for anyone desiring to hear and communicate God's voice. I am deeply moved every time I experience Shawn Bolz's ministry, and I am excited that, through this book, we all will learn how to access God's secrets too. Many blessings,

EDWINA FINDLEY
Hollywood Actress
edwinafindley.com

I have known Shawn Bolz for many years and it has been a great honor to watch him grow in the Lord and in his prophetic gift. In the last few years, I have seen him step into something new in revelation like I've never seen before. Shawn walks powerfully in words of knowledge, which is a sign and wonder in itself. The way he operates in this gift changes lives as the people receiving his ministry experience the tangible love of the Father. In *God Secrets*, Shawn shares practical steps for growing in this gift and inspires us to hunger for the revelation of heaven, to know God's secrets, and to live a life filled with the beauty of words of knowledge. I highly recommend this book to anyone who wants to grow in revelation and bring people into encounters with our very loving Father!

KRIS VALLOTTON

Senior Associate Leader, Bethel Church, Redding CA

Co-founder of the Bethel School of Supernatural Ministry

Author of 13 books, including *The Supernatural Ways of Royalty* and *Destined to Win*

krisvallotton.com

The best endorsement I can give is this, I cried through the whole book! There is nothing like the word of knowledge that conveys the love of God to an individual soul. Will I ever be able to forget AzusaNow 2016, when Shawn called out people's names and situations from a crowd of seventy thousand people? Oh the love of God! I was blown away. All I can say about Shawn— his love, his gift, and this book—is to quote John Wesley, "When will this kind of Christianity fill the whole earth?"

LOU ENGLE

The Call

www.thecall.com

It's a special thing when you have a friend who operates in a unique prophetic gift. It's unreal when that friend is able to activate people into the same gift. I have experienced this more times than I can count—of seeing people step into words of knowledge after hearing Shawn speak or after reading one of his books. There is a promotion that takes place and it has brought much joy to me to see our global family step into this.

ERIC JOHNSON

Bethel Redding Author, *Momentum* and *Christ in You*

www.bethel.com

Shawn Bolz has done a great service to the body of Christ with this eminently worthy book on the word of knowledge. I have been involved in most every move of God in my almost seventy-two years of apostolic ministry and it seems so little has been said or even known about the word of knowledge. I recall in the early years of the voice of healing movement that it was always called the gift of the discerning of spirits. On one occasion not too many years ago, Oral Roberts and I were at dinner discussing William Branham's word of knowledge gift, which was the inspiration for Oral to enter the healing ministry. As we spoke, Oral reached over, took my wrist, and said, "Brother Paul, I never had the gift of the word of knowledge like you and Brother Branham." I had the pleasure of correcting him by relating some outstanding instances in which he did indeed use the gift of the word of knowledge. His face glowed. He then said, "Well, I really did use the gift without knowing, but I called it the gift of discernment." Now, thanks to Shawn and this great work, no one should be remiss insofar as the use of the word of knowledge. This book gives us a taste of it, that we might continue to seek for it.

PAUL CAIN
Evangelist
www.paulcainministries.wordpress.com

Shawn Bolz is obeying the 1 Corinthian 14:1 mandate to follow the way of love and earnestly desire spiritual gifts. But he'll be the first to tell you he had to press in, practice, and discover how to flow accurately. He had to train his senses to discern the good coming from God's heart (see Hebrews 5:14). In his latest book, Shawn gives you the practical instruction and encouragement you need to be what he calls a prophetic risk-taker—one who is more concerned about sharing God's love with others than about embarrassing oneself. This book will help you sharpen your skills as you pursue God's heart for people through the gift of words of wisdom. I highly recommend this book!

JENNIFER LECLAIRE
Senior Editor, Charisma magazine
Senior Leader, Awakening House of Prayer
Author, *The Making of a Prophet*
www.jenniferleclaire.org

The first time I heard of Shawn was around seven years ago through the most incredible encounter and word of knowledge that he had for me! Shawn was walking on Hollywood Boulevard when Jesus appeared to him and said, "Go into a tourist shop in the area and buy Wendy a key ring with the word 'Hollywood' and pictures of cameras on it!" Shawn did exactly that; and even though he didn't know me, he wrote me a card about apostolically breaking through the entertainment gate and how many would eventually follow. Through a mutual friend, the key ring and card came into my hands and it is the project Chronicles of Brothers that we are developing for HW right now! It was after this that we met in Los Angeles and became friends. Oh, and Shawn lives a totally surrendered life that is marked indelibly by love. There are very few people I have encountered who have the capacity to love people in every walk of life from the highest echelons of society to the totally broken. The hallmark of his ministry is love. When the prophet Bob Jones went to glory, something incredible happened to Shawn. The words of knowledge he has been operating in, truly I believe, is one of the rarest and most unique gifts on the earth today and is fueled by one thing alone: Jesus' love for people. I believe this is the Father's new and unique mantle on Shaun. But I do believe that Bob Jones, who loved Shawn for so many years, is watching out for him from Glory! This book is one we so desperately need as Christians in the earth today. Thank you, thank you, dear Shawn, for writing it. It is right on time and such an encouragement to all of us to press through in this gift when so many are so broken and desperate to know that the Father sees. Your love and gift are impacting the world for Jesus! Thank you for your incredible obedience to the call.

WENDY ALEC

Co-founder, GOD TV Creative Director, Warboys Entertainment, London
Author, *Chronicles of Brothers*
www.chroniclesofbrothers.com

As a businesswoman who has depended heavily upon words of knowledge, discernment and the prophetic in order to be able to do the things I'm called to do in my personal and CEO life, Shawn's book (and ministry!) is a breath of fresh air! The prophetic doesn't fit into a box, and I was encountering God on the pages of *God Secrets* as very out-of-the-box exciting, events were relayed! It took me to a deeper understanding of how to further use what I know and how to step into new levels my heart has been crying out for. Shawn is such a blessing for this generation that craves relationship and authenticity!

SANDI KRAKOWSKI

President and CEO, A Real Change International, Inc.Direct marketing copywriter, author, business consultant and speaker
www.arealchange.com

CONTENTS

FOREWORD

BY GRAHAM COOKE

The recurring themes in this excellent book are the constant messages of scripture for the prophetic lifestyle in a new covenant culture.

The intentionality of God's heart, mind and will. The development of a close personal relationship with the Father through the ever constant presence of the Lord Jesus. The continual confirmation of the loving disposition of God towards humanity.

The preparation required to step out in faith. The need to take risks in what you believe. The focus on abiding in Jesus and maintaining a connection with the Holy Spirit. The development of a healthy New Testament relational theology in who Jesus is for us in the new man, and what He has accomplished for our freedom from the old.

Life in the Spirit is about cultivating wisdom in the Secret Place of God's heart. To know how He truly sees people. To know the process of the innermost thoughts of God that moves divine perspectives into spiritual appraisal, releasing a kingdom language that empowers people to feel known by their Creator. All from a place of perfect safety in Christ, in whom is hidden all the treasures of wisdom and knowledge.

The foundation of all ministry is a profound gratitude in the unchanging nature of God. A hunger and thirst to be with the Three in every circumstance. To have total confidence in the genius Holy Spirit and His love for the Lord Jesus. To experience the astonishing focus of Jesus on His Father as He pursues all that He is saying and doing. To love the learning that is present in all of our life situations. This book is full of wisdom in the development of such a relational and ministerial profile.

In a ministry where all mistakes are public, the key to longevity is humility. Shawn's openly honest approach to his ministry is both refreshing and instructive. Only the teachable can teach effectively. His confidence in God's goodness is the springboard for the release of God's gift and the freedom it creates in people.

The book is a massive example of a humble man looking out from within God's nature to connect people to Him and His word. Every time I read the Gospels I see the same God-like example in Jesus. A heart relationship with God is the doorway to encounter and experience for other people. I have seen too many examples of the opposite; people pursuing gifts for power and influence, the leaders and ministries who leverage their position for the purpose of control and recognition.

Shawn draws you into a place of excitement and truth. You don't have to be "special." Ordinary people in touch and in tune with an extraordinary God can fulfill a high calling in the Kingdom. One-dimensional people walking with a multidimensional God who will always take up the slack, that's the difference and the breeding ground for humility.

As people are discipled in a humble life, their language is first trusting and confident; "I think, I believe that God is saying something." In the cauldron of public learning, it is both sensible and humble to ask questions. "Is there a John here from Columbus?" Only a humble heart can keep us one step removed from pressure. In story after story, Shawn shows us the lifestyle required to live in the heat of the furnace that is the public ministry of the supernatural.

As our conviction about reliance on God's relationship with us grows, we progress to faith and confidence where the more powerful, revelatory truth resides. Our ministry becomes a beautiful ebb and flow between trust and faith. The difference between our delight in Him and the fullness of His joy in us. Shawn epitomizes a man and a ministry on such a journey. I quote, "Be open to failure. The key thing is to meet your personal ministry goal of loving the person." Love people too much not to share God's heart for them. It is never about us. It is only about who God is for us, in us and through us.

Pursuing spiritual gifts earnestly is code for practicing loads! Pay attention to how your ministry affects you. If you were accurate, how did that feel to you? If you missed it, what was happening? Learn the presence aspect. Be aware of the stress that leads to striving. This book provides excellent advice about how to avoid performance pressure.

Shawn's public secret is his love of intimacy and sensitivity to the Three. He avoids the need to be spectacular and presents himself as ordinary. Being alive to God makes us more aware of people. Jesus is the door to a new experience and encounter. Supernatural gifts are the handle of the Holy Spirit opening up space in Jesus for God to speak and to act.

Chapters 3 and 4 should be required study for all people who are being discipled. They are the very frameworks for growing in these specific gifts. They are, however, quite useless without the rest of the book, which is the constant revelation of who God is in Himself and how we can be known and loved by Him personally.

There are counterfeit ministries across the five-fold spectrum from pastors to apostles. There are also counterfeit "investigators," normally known as trolls who weave a web of lies and misinterpretation from a negative mindset (expressly forbidden in scripture). Often, their burden of proof arises out of their own lack of doctrinal clarity evidenced by their opposition to the New Testament Church.

Persecution of people living in fullness is nothing new, and in this book Shawn demonstrates an admirable restraint. To meet an accusation with an accusation is to do the work of the accuser. Jesus is the public defender of His own body. If people are intent on sowing judgment, it is better to reap judgment now, whilst they can still repent and be changed, rather than in the afterlife, where new is no longer an option.

I love so many truths, examples and practices in this book. I particularly like the element concerning the ministry difference between Christian and pre-Christian. Pre-Christians make mistakes in life because they have no relationship with God and no access to wisdom or revelatory truth, which produces and maintains freedom. It is a profound joy to see God open a door for them to step into a new spiritual space.

However, much of prophetic, revelatory ministry is spent on Christians who have never been taught to hear God's voice. They have not been taught how to live in the new man but have actively been discipled to live in the sin-conscious culture of the old. They struggle with negative thoughts, emotions, perspectives and language. They come to the prophetic ministry expecting to receive a word that they could hear for themselves if they were taught effectively. Meanwhile, there is a world out there desperately in need of revelation, intentional love and divine intervention.

Shawn is a New Testament prophet, marked by Jesus in the new man. A man of love, goodness, gentleness and humility—attributes which are as alive in his writing as they are in his. Taken together, these attributes are the most feared by the enemy as they are denied by the religious minded.

Therefore, this makes them the most real, profound and marvelous vehicle for the gifts of the Spirit. Walking with God is the most wonderful experience ever and new covenant prophets draw people into that same place of wonder. I hope you hear the love, humility, curiosity and wonder in Shawn's writing.

How I wish that I had access in the early 1970s to this level of wisdom, perspective and practical insight into how to move in the gifts of prophecy and words of knowledge. When I started in this ministry, there were few who knew how to do it, steward it, or disciple people in it.

I wept for myself and all I was forced to endure as an introvert thrust into the harsh spotlight of a platform created only for extroverts. I cried for friends who were destroyed by other people's ignorance and superstition, some who took their own life because the relentless opposition proved too great. Others who succumbed to the spiritual PTSD of its day, the constant clamoring within the church of people seeing you as the instant fix for all their problems.

In that context alone, this book is highly important. In the context of developing people in a culture of intimacy and sensitivity to the Presence of God, this book is invaluable.

It should be required reading for any type of spiritual school or training program.

The lifestyle of the man and the ministry who wrote this book demonstrates what is required in the pursuit of spiritual gifts.

GRAHAM COOKE
www.brilliantperspectives.com

INTRODUCTION

I love that Christianity and our faith are based on this amazing reality that God interacts with us. All of Scripture is filled with these unbelievable stories, where everyday human beings are brought into the greatness of a real connection to God.

I am especially inspired by the stories of God speaking to His people and how all of it plays out for His glory. I love watching what He can do in our lives through His beautiful interactions. Many of these expressive stories come through gifts of the Holy Spirit that unfortunately are often misunderstood and barely pursued today.

I grew up in an environment of people who passionately pursued God and desired to hear Him. In our church, I saw the power of words of knowledge, especially through healing. Someone would hear God and identify a sickness or physical problem, and then we would all pray for healing. However, these moments were rare, even for our progressive church.

At times, a few notable figures we all looked up to would bring an atmosphere of awe through their faith to connect with God's voice.

They would stand there, pounding out a row of revelatory words, as they spoke to various individuals in the crowd. Through divine revelation, they identified sicknesses and shared words based on names for people they had never met. The gifts and ministry of these men and women have always fascinated me. Throughout my life, I've pursued this gift of receiving these kinds of revelatory words for the people around me.

As a child, I didn't know the difference between a prophecy, a word of knowledge, an interpretation of tongues, or a word of wisdom—they all seemed just clumped together as those strange gifts that only a few people operated in and enjoyed. In fact, it seemed like most of the people who had a reputation in these areas were strange and a little socially awkward. Honestly, I almost got stuck in that mindset as I looked at the people who were representing these great gifts. But thankfully, Scripture always showed me something different. I remember reading stories from the Bible and thinking, *"But then there is Jesus who is our example, and His stories are so alive."* And then I'd read the amazing stories I could relate to about people who heard from God—like Mary and Joseph, the apostle Paul, and Jesus' disciples like Peter and John. If there wasn't interaction, faith just felt so empty to me.

So, I have pursued a life of communication with God. I wasn't born with a gift, and I didn't have a moment in my youth where an angel visited me as when Gabriel came to Mary. I just followed biblical examples, especially from Jesus, who gave us some of the greatest pictures of what words of knowledge from heaven could do.

Prophecy is an awesome gift that God has shared with us to give us hints or direct messages about the future and our lives. Through faith, the messages we receive can help us position our lives for something God wants to do in and through us. Words of wisdom are so useful because they help you understand how to apply what God is saying or doing in you to speak or relate to the world around you. But words of knowledge are my favorite. I am a guy who loves quality time, and words of knowledge cause me to feel like the omnipresent God is choosing to be with me in that moment.

Words of knowledge ground you in the truth that God knows you, and He loves you. Hearing His purpose for our lives causes a moment of wonder and awe as we witness the nature of God's love and nurturing care put on display for everyone to see. This is like the awe that David shares for his all-knowing creator in Psalm 139:1-7 (The Message):

> God, investigate my life; get all the facts firsthand. I'm an open book to you; even from a distance, you know what I'm thinking. You know when I leave or when I get back; I'm never out of your sight. You know everything I'm going to say before I start the first sentence. I look behind me and you're there, then up ahead and you're there too—your reassuring presence, coming and going. This is too much, too wonderful—I can't take it all in! Is there anyplace I can go to avoid your Spirit? To be out of your sight?

When the God of all creation speaks to *you*, life is now different. The most powerful person in the universe knows you and loves you. He cares for you. As David says, it is "too much, too wonderful." The world inside you changes.

I wrote the book *Translating God* to help bring people into a love-based approach to prophetic ministry and revelation pursuit. I hope this book will help you to understand and then prioritize a life pursuing gifts of revelation—especially sharing the knowledge of God directly from His mind and heart!

A FOUNDATION FOR
WORDS OF KNOWLEDGE

couldn't believe I was taking the largest platform of my life.

Sixty-five-thousand people had gathered (in addition to hundreds of thousands watching on TV) to commemorate what had happened roughly one hundred years before on Azusa Street—the revival signaling the birth of Pentecostalism. I was invited to be part of this historic event, The Call, that was all about asking God to do something big again in our generation.

Months before, the directors of the event invited me to take the stage for possibly one of the longer sections of the night to model prophetic gifts and then to ask God to empower others to do the same. I was excited to be asked to play a small part. I had been seeing some really wonderful implementation of spiritual gifts, specifically words of knowledge, and knew that though they have always been available to us, they were a new concept to the vast majority of the body of Christ.

On the day of the event (April 9, 2016), however, I was a little less excited. I had almost nothing to say! I had been praying for weeks asking God for anything, trying to surrender my heart for that moment. Usually I get clues, thoughts, or even just one-word hints, to write down in advance. But nothing came.

An hour before I was supposed to take the stage, I told the event leadership that I didn't have any strong impressions and suggested that they skip my time because I hadn't heard anything that felt big enough to take a step of faith in front of such a large audience. They refused and told me that they would love for me to try no matter what.

Then I got caught up in a worship song (one of many playing that day), and I felt all of my self-driven performance expectations falling off me. I focused on my primary purpose for being a part of the event: to love Jesus and to love people. Jesus' love for me felt so good in that moment that I forgot about everything else. That's when a few words came into my heart and mind. Just a few, but they felt like they could be something. I'll describe the process later, but just know that I was as surprised as everyone else in the crowd. Here I had prayed for months for anything, and in just a simple act of loving on Him and falling in love with the crowd, something happened.

I know lots of ministry people who are full of confidence, but that was not me that day. I wasn't that confident when I took the platform. I had my notes on my cell phone. I knew that might look bad to people who didn't understand or believe in prophecy, but I needed the frame of reference, and the rain that had filled the stadium had wrecked any possibility of using an actual journal. We live in a technology age though, so I am always using a phone or an iPad to write my notes.

I shared my first word in a question, asking the crowd about a few specific details that described someone's life—words of knowledge that would need to line up with someone there.

"Is there a Kenneth Ray and Patricia Lou who came together?"

I asked people to raise and wave their hands high in the air to let me know if anyone was here that matched these words. Remember, we're talking about a crowd of sixty-five-thousand people, and I'm looking for four waving arms.

The crowd began to look around as well. These words were so specific that I knew either this man and woman were there, or this wasn't God—that's a way to take a risk in front of a massive group of people. I heard screaming and shouting, as throughout the crowd people pointed toward a couple who were waving their hands. Everyone got really excited together. They were a married couple and my words were their first and middle names. Then I asked about four other names, which were the names of four out of their five kids. We all went wild together knowing that this was God!

"God is healing a list of needs in your body that you incurred from the mission field," I told Patricia.

In what felt like inspiration from the Holy Spirit, I told her that God was sending her family back to Oregon. (Even some of their closest friends didn't know about this upcoming move.) I shared a street that Patricia had lived on when she was young. Long story short, God spoke to their family about where they were at, the direction they were headed, and how they were going to impact the world as a family.

The venue turned into a living room; we were all in this together. We laughed when this couple responded together out of pure joy. We celebrated that God was healing Patricia. We were excited when the word about the move came. It was a moment in time when we all had so much faith that God had just blown in like a wind and did something only He could do. After several more words, I prayed for the crowd to eagerly desire to prophesy.

I believe that for a good majority of people who were there, we saw a new hunger emerge for revelation that day. Somehow, my small model during my fifteen minutes caused a ripple of excitement, hope, and anticipation that God can speak, and when He does it is really useful and exciting. Some described how they were in shock and others talked about being in awe of who God was in a way that had just never hit them before. I realized I was supposed to be a bridge to this amazing congregation that had gathered. I modeled what could be considered a new prototype of revelation and then released impartation and faith that I hope you, too, will gain from this book.

I want to be a living bridge between what you have heard about others doing and actually accessing it yourself, to help you believe that you can share things God shows you and hear God in very real ways! He wants to tell you His secrets!

A PRAYER FOR GREATER MEASURE

Ten years ago, I had the privilege of spending time with Paul Cain, a leader in the great spiritual revivals in the 1950s. I listened intently as Paul shared some of his favorite stories from his long life of ministry. I had witnessed Paul give hundreds of words to people, and one thing that really marked the experience was how he included words of knowledge that gave very real details of people's lives, causing them to feel God's presence and, just know He was there.

But this time as Paul shared, I just had faith. I had been pursuing ministry for years, but Paul's unique experiences with specifically hearing God's voice made me so hungry to be more practical and relevant to the world around me. This hunger came from seeing the direct impact that more specific prophecy could bring. Before, when I had observed this, I thought accessing it was based on how gifted you are, but now something had changed in me. I had a revelation through reading the Bible and seeing this example that this was accessible to every one of us.

The way I saw Paul minister was very down to earth and authentic. I wanted to ask Paul to pray for me to see if I could operate like him. I wanted God to use me through words of knowledge in the same way He used Paul.

I think of King Saul who went to Shiloh where the prophets were gathered and how Saul prophesied powerfully, just like they did, because he got under the Spirit of God that the prophets carried. Saul had an impartation or an experience of grace—just from being with the prophets (God's messengers) in this place (see 1 Sam. 10:10-11).

Now Paul's story is dynamic. His mother almost died of several debilitating diseases when she was carrying him, but an angel came to her and said, "Don't worry, you will have a son named Paul" and then spoke of Paul's ministry calling. Paul was a very special signpost to the world around him, and he was very rare in his generation. At one point, he had the largest tent revival meetings for healing, in addition to a popular TV show. He met with kings, presidents, dictators, and politicians who were eager to hear what God might say to them through him. We haven't seen many like Paul, if any, on this earth.

I, on the other hand, am normal; my mom and dad just had me. I wasn't born under a sign or with any extraordinary sense of a solitary purpose. I have never been one of the cool people or one of the best … but I have been a good person who loves well. When I asked Paul to pray for me, I knew it was a long shot to receive what he had. I was already regularly pursuing prophecy because in his first letter to the Corinthians, the apostle Paul tells us to go after love as if our lives depended on it and to "eagerly desire gifts of the Spirit, especially prophecy" (1 Cor. 14:1). I have always loved seeing how God uses our willingness and desire to share our faith to do something special in all of our lives. I have always been hungry to see God come through these amazing moments of prophecy and revelation. But this man, Paul Cain, was on another level that just seemed unattainable.

Paul agreed to pray for me, and he shared something that God showed him.

"You are a token to a generation, a vessel of God to show them what is possible," Paul told me. "You, Shawn, will be a bridge to our generation. When people see your gift, they will believe that they can do it too, and run across your faith into prophesying powerfully! God is going to give you more because you will give it away!"

ANOTHER PROVIDENTIAL MEETING

Five years after Paul prophesied over me, I met a man named James Maloney who was extremely gifted in the revelatory gifts. At our first meeting, I watched as he ministered to someone and described, for fifteen minutes, this person's life framework. Our time together was so significant, and we ended up holding quite a few meetings together.

What James did was so detailed. One time, he told someone he could see his desk and a real estate contract on it and that he wasn't supposed to sell to the government. He knew how many children this man had and was able to share advice for his family. Then, through a word of knowledge, he prophesied a medical condition. There was so much faith that the man was instantly healed!

I was amazed! One of our meetings together was in New Mexico. James called me up to pray for me. He had one of his revelation experiences, a series of visions, words of knowledge, and what he called a "full-motion movie screen" in front of his eyes. He talked about a car accident I had been in that left me with lingering back issues. He even knew how old I was when it happened and the color of the car. I was instantly healed. Since then, I've never felt that same back pain. Then, even more awesomely, James said to me, "You will move to a higher level of revelation and release others to do so. You will have words like I am getting in my visionary experiences" (he uses the word "panorama" to describe his experience). As he spoke, I could feel power come into my spirit.

I knew God was setting up my faith for more, but I also knew I didn't want to just move in the prophetic in a more specific or powerful way. I wanted to see this generation embrace this powerful tool of revelation.

Here I was, this guy who had received prophecy for my life by amazing men of God—twice. I loved the word Paul gave me! It gave me so much faith. James's prophetic word was also transformational. But five years after James ministered to me, it was business as usual each time I practiced sharing what God was showing me. That's not to say there weren't wonderful moments. Pursuing something out of faithfulness that God really wants for you and gives you grace for is beautiful. But Paul's and James' prayers had led me to believe in more.

As is usually the case in life, when I did get the release of a greater measure of words of knowledge, I wasn't anticipating it. These spiritual gifts and my pursuit toward them were still a part of me, but my season of life—my new marriage, our first child, our pastoral role at our church, our business, etc.—kept the greater level of faith to do more with these gifts on the back-burner of my heart. When these gifts exploded inside me, I wasn't prepared and was the one who least expected it.

I want to share with you what I have learned from living a lifestyle of pursuing God's secrets, especially when it comes to words of knowledge and revelation. I believe these personal insights will not only be helpful and interesting, but my hope and prayer is for them to also empower your own faith.

INTENTIONALITY TO KNOW GOD'S HEART, MIND, AND WILL

I have been living a life of intentionality toward developing a closeness to God. One of the most dynamic parts of this has been my pursuit of the prophetic gifts. I know that they confirm the very love nature of God, so I have set my life to see what could happen if I just took risks with what I believe is from God. Focusing on connection to the Holy Spirit and going after healthy theology about who Jesus is creates the most amazing foundation for becoming a receptor of revelation. Because the prophetic gifts are the only ones that Paul told all of us to "eagerly desire," I'm convinced we can successfully pursue them and discover a thriving life of revelation.

Christianity at large believes that God is speaking. We believe He wants to direct us in our lives and help us to know Him and His will for our lives. At times, the word "prophecy" gets a little controversial in some parts of the church world, but it has become increasingly accepted. However, words of knowledge are rarer in the church, except for in some groups that pursue healing ministry (prayer for supernatural healing). Words of knowledge are not just about hearing God in the context of prophecy or healing. The gift of words of knowledge gives us the ability to know what's going on in the inner workings of God's mind. And when we know what's happening in God's mind and heart, we have the ability to seek His will with clarity in every aspect of our lives and world. Knowing His will can affect your family and change your business. It can change education; it can even reform politics.

GOD HAS SECRETS TO SHARE WITH US!

God has thoughts and intentions towards each one of us, towards our family, towards this earth, towards governments and towards occupations. Scripture tells us that He discloses His secrets to those He trusts. He relates information (His secrets) about other people and groups—secrets that reshape the direction of someone's life or a government's reign.

Words of knowledge come when God wants to deposit His intimate knowledge inside our hearts and minds, embedding it into our perspective. I will go into this much more in upcoming chapters, but for now I want to invite you to start this journey with me: What if God wants to have the kind of relationship with you that lets you in on His secrets? What if you start to hear His innermost thoughts?

In today's church, words of knowledge have been one of the least pursued of the revelatory gifts, and yet they are among the most powerful gifts that believers can practice. The gift of getting knowledge from divine revelation helps define an aha moment that tells us, "God is real, He is here, and He loves you." It creates space for people to be in awe and even shocked by who God is and how intimately He loves them in the midst of all of humanity. Because all of humanity passionately seeks after knowledge and information about our lives, knowledge becomes one of the most valuable expressions of God's revelatory gifts.

Words of knowledge sound so simple but bring with them a full encounter with the God of all the universe as He tells us His secrets. To the person who receives the word, they cause the ever-present God to manifest Himself in the here and now.

WHAT IS A BIBLICAL WORD OF KNOWLEDGE?

To one there is given through the Spirit a message of wisdom, to another a message of knowledge by means of the same Spirit (1 Cor. 12:8).

So many people get confused about what they're pursuing when they think of a "word of knowledge" and then just wind up clumping everything together as "prophecy." A word of knowledge is actually a very different part of the revelation gift. Let me give you some simple explanations that I think will help as you dive deeper into this wondrous gift.

PROPHECY is a word about the future that shows the plans that God has for someone or a group/region/business, etc. With prophecy, people's affections lie in the fact that God knows them and has plans for them. Knowing God's plans and future for their lives gives people the opportunity to partner with Him to actually see those plans fulfilled.

WORDS OF WISDOM are actual pieces of wisdom that come to us to help us know how to apply our plans and even other prophetic words to our lives. When it is a word, wisdom is like an instruction. Think of it as heaven coaching you on how to plan and pursue who you are or what you're called to, or how to love those who are your destiny.

A WORD OF KNOWLEDGE includes supernatural revelation by the Holy Spirit about something that is important to God. While not solely discerned, the information includes specific facts that will help bring God's knowledge through a manifest form into your life or into the life of someone you're ministering to and sharing God's heart.

If the word of knowledge is for individuals, it will bring their hearts closer to the mind of God. This type of revelation helps people know what God is thinking and what is important and valuable to them.

Words of knowledge help people feel known by God, compelling them to believe more deeply in the truth. In fact, it creates a moment that causes a feeling of awe or wonder in how intricately God is involved and cares. A word makes who Jesus is and the sacrifice He made on the cross so alive. It's one of those black-and-white moments with no hint of doubt or uncertainty.

To bring the faith needed for its release, a word of knowledge can come right before a prophecy, healing, or miracle because the word is so specific or in tune with what's happening right then. In other words, the one true and living God addresses or acknowledges whatever is the deepest desire or concern in your heart. He seems to say, "I love this person more than you do," or, "I am here, and I will help you."

Words of knowledge can bring faith for wisdom or application for revelation. In Colossians 2:3, Paul tells us, "In Christ are hidden all the treasures of wisdom and knowledge." Words of knowledge help us to treasure who Jesus is and apply this nature to our everyday life. It is a revelation in the moment of the knowledge that is in Christ.

Back in the early days of God's people, knowing someone in a biblical sense meant you had a deep intimacy with them. In fact, the Hebrew word (*yada*) for "know" or "knowledge" meant sexual intimacy. This ministry isn't about gaining information; it's about having intimate knowledge of the mind and heart of God.

We see one of the clearest pictures of how God downloaded natural and spiritual knowledge in the life and book of Daniel. Chapter 1 tells us that Daniel and his young friends received spiritual knowledge and understanding of literature and learning (verse 17). Through words of knowledge, God helped them advise the king and his kingdom.

God wants us to major on taking risks with the prophetic and our words because they help people feel fully known and connected to God.

By the way, you don't need to boil down all of these terms and definitions into a science, but I will say that the more you understand what you're doing, the more you can partner your faith in the different aspects of the prophetic gifts. If you want to learn about all of the spiritual gifts, start with my first book, *Translating God,* or read some of Graham Cooke's or James Maloney's amazing materials.

As you read this book, I want to encourage you to see God in His wonderful gift of words of knowledge and to pursue interaction with Him in this way. Set this as one of your spiritual goals. In the days to come, Christians who begin to hear God's mind and heart about current events, people's past experiences, and all things in between will be one of the most valuable resources for counseling the world at large.

JESUS REVEALS GOD'S NATURE

Through simple words of knowledge and prophetic wisdom, Jesus gained whole audiences of influence. Think about His interaction with Zacchaeus, the hated tax collector. This stocky, short man wanted an audience with Jesus so much that he climbed up into a sycamore tree to just try and see Him. What he didn't know is that God wanted to meet with him even more than Zacchaeus desired to see the Savior. Our friend Zac was hoping to get the attention of this Jesus who seemed so authentic. He thought He might just be who everyone said He was. But he knew he would probably be passed by.

Then it happens: Jesus looks up to see Zacchaeus hanging out in a tree and calls to him by name: "Zacchaeus, come down and prepare your house for a visit from Me!"

Like any of us who have been called by that voice of love, which says a thousand things using very few words, Zacchaeus was shocked, thrilled and scared—all at the same time. But he knew it was *his* time. Some of the religious people in the crowd slandered him to Jesus: "Don't go and be with that crook, that unworthy man! If you knew him, you would never set foot in his house."

Not wanting to miss the opportunity, Zacchaeus defended himself, but Jesus validated him, saying, "I am coming, don't worry." Jesus wasn't looking at the natural. He was sharing the affections, love and vision of His Father for this man who may have been little, but held so much significance to the God of all the universe, and in that moment, Zacchaeus felt it. He was known by name to the man who came from heaven. Life would never be the same!

Think of all the people who took in this moment, especially those who felt unworthy of connection to God and others. In that one revelatory moment, Jesus showed hundreds, if not thousands, of people that they were loved, and that they mattered. Suddenly, they had hope for a chance to be connected to God.

Throughout the Gospels, we see Jesus get words of knowledge that aren't really about knowing someone's name or information. His words validated a person's identity and made them feel significant to God Himself. Everyone knew Zacchaeus in that town or area. He was the chief tax collector, known for his crooked business practices. But the moment that changed his life forever likely rebranded Zacchaeus in many of their hearts. As they saw Jesus care for him, Zacchaeus's identity transformed in their eyes. They saw him as a person, not just as a necessary evil.

I can only think that this word of knowledge caused a spiritual climate shift in Jericho, and it was such a simple word! Those who complained about Zacchaeus had two choices: (1) change their opinion of him, or (2) change their opinion about Jesus.

If you pursue words of knowledge, you'll realize that the gift of knowing the thoughts of God shifts the lens you see people and culture through. Words of knowledge validate God's love for people that others may not see in that light. In fact, getting God's knowledge actually gives you the eyes to see things you would never have even looked at without His perspective. It's like seeing another color that no one knew existed.

I have exciting news for you: *If you pursue them, you will grow in words of knowledge!* They are a gift that we can develop just like any other spiritual gift. I'm writing this book to give you faith, a real-life model, and Scripture for your own journey with the voice of God. I want to see you run after this amazing experiential gift that makes the world feel so known and loved by our Father who is in heaven. I want to help set you up for a successful approach where the primary goal is not really about operating in a gift as much as it is about knowing God's heart. The gift serves your connection with God.

But just like pursuing relationship is never a five-step process, hearing God is connected to knowing God, and that will take more than just giving you definitions. I hope your heart and mind will be prepared to pursue the culture of God's heart. This sets the foundation for hearing words of knowledge and teaches us how to walk out an amazing prophetic journey. We begin to understand how to relate God to the world around us.

THE YELLOW RAIN JACKET

One of the things I love about words of knowledge is the way God uses them to affirm something someone may already be sensing. One of my favorite times was a few years ago. I was in the backseat of a car on the way to a dinner to meet some of my family's friends. It was a harmless little social gathering just to share food and connect.

I was playing a game on my phone when I saw a picture in my mind's eye. In my head, I could clearly see my friends named James and Susan. The mental image stayed, and pretty soon I realized it wasn't just a random memory coming up. God was trying to get my attention.

"God, are You trying to tell me something?" I asked, still focusing on the image.

That's when I received what I felt was a direct feed from the heart and mind of God for a different James and Susan. I immediately had knowledge about them. It's hard to explain, but it was like I was sharing so deeply in God's thoughts that they felt organic to my own. What was in His imagination and thoughts had merged with my own. So much of what we see are word pictures in our head. That's what happened in this moment.

I could see two children, named Olivia and Sam, and this small family struggling financially. And then I could see a yellow rain jacket. I had no idea what these thoughts were, but I could feel they belonged to some of the people I was meeting that night. I began to pray and hoped that I'd have an opportunity to ask and possibly pray for them about this feed of revelation that was so disconnected from my natural knowledge of them.

The good friends we were meeting had brought another couple to tag along with us at dinner. I was glad to meet this beautiful couple but knew this wasn't just a nice social gathering when they told me their names: Jim (James) and Sue (Susan)! I really didn't know what to do with my experience in the car, so I just waited and enjoyed our time together.

We had a great night just socializing, and at one point this couple mentioned they had kids but didn't really say much about them. Their words inspired me to take a risk. I thought to myself, "If someone had something precious to say that might give me hope for my kids, I would want them to take the risk". I mustered the courage to speak and said to our small group, "Guys, can I hijack the conversation for a second to have a spiritual moment? I know we are all Christians here, but I wanted to know if I could share a spiritual impression I felt from God about your family?" They seemed open to it, acting as if it was completely normal for them to do this kind of thing, even though I knew it wasn't.

"Are your kids' names Olivia and Samuel?" I asked.

They smiled and nodded, trying to figure out how I knew this. I knew they assumed my friend had told me. My hosts knew I didn't know their children's names and were enjoying the prophetic moment.

"I feel like God is showing me that you have been through the hardest financial battle of your life but that He is with you and is going to help you, especially with Olivia and Sam. There is provision for them to live out their life full of education and also life experience. God wants to give you epic trips, like your European vacation and your family trip to Israel, again."

"I then saw a yellow rain jacket, and it was being folded up and had a price tag on it. I saw it selling for a really high price and saw you guys walking into a huge manufacturing plant with plans for a new, way better rain jacket that had global distribution."

They sat in shock. Sue was crying lightly. "Does the rain jacket mean something to you?" I asked. They nodded and explained that they were part owners in a company called Rain Jacket. They were currently in a lawsuit with other owners, which had been ruining their lives. They had been praying about selling their share and starting something else. They were wonderful Christians who were praying about this situation, but they didn't know they could hear from God about it. Bottom line, though, was that their gut (I would call it their spiritual "know-er") told them that they had a whole world of opportunity ahead of them if they sold their company. But they didn't know how to take that risky step, even though they believed it was the right thing to do.

Now, through this word, they knew God was saying He was with them, that He cared about their family, that He loved their children by name, and that they could recreate their success on a broader level. They knew that God approved of their desire for a truly good life and that the prophetic word had even mentioned trips they had enjoyed. They knew now they could take that risk.

"I haven't felt this good or light in two years," Jim said. "Actually, I don't know if I have ever felt like God was so close to me."

Sue shared how she had been devastated that they were going to have to take the kids out of their school next year because they couldn't afford it any longer. She looked so relieved about their life and future.

I love how God loves through words of knowledge.

GOD MANIFESTS HIS PRESENCE IN THE NOW!

From the time I was young, I saw how an accurate word of knowledge could change a person's life. One word could totally bring the God who is supernatural and omnipresent into an experience where He manifests His presence in the now of someone's life. We know He is everywhere all at once, which in some ways seems impersonal to a generation who longs to be so connected to Him. Then there is the beautiful fact that Jesus, in John 16, promised us a relationship with the Father like the one He has through the Holy Spirit—the Spirit that can manifest the omnipresent God in the "right now" moments of our lives.

God chooses to come into our days and visit. I love Psalm 118:24: "This is the day that the Lord has made, and I will rejoice and be glad in it." This verse so describes how we're supposed to live so well. The mercies of God are new every morning, and each of the days we live are vessels that our huge, infinite God uses to fill time and space with His goodness. As we get to know Him, we start to know what is inside His heart and mind for us in the now.

When we expect God to be in the here and now, we realize that our moments can and should be influenced by Him. Have you lost your keys? He knows where they are and can help you. Need help making a hard decision? He can plant His knowledge and wisdom deep in your heart. We're believing in a relationship with God that has extreme spiritual implications, but that also impacts our everyday practical life. Engaging with the gift of words of knowledge will connect you to Him in profound ways through the mundane days of life.

If you read my previous book, *Translating God*, you know that my passion and calling is to use stories, examples, philosophy, and theology to convey specific principles that help us see the God secrets around us. The prophetic gifts have been one of the most misunderstood subjects, so to try and quantify them is no simple task. I hope you'll get the marvelous courage to try words of knowledge. If you do, you just might change the world. My workbooks provide the "how to," but this book is meant to wind your heart down a trail of connection with God, setting the right goal for these pursuits.

In the next chapter, we'll look at some of the attributes and characteristics of a life filled with words of knowledge.

2

THE BEAUTY OF A LIFE FILLED WITH WORDS OF KNOWLEDGE

love how God takes a few of our spiritual thoughts, or inspires our imagination with spiritual ideas and images, and ultimately makes a beautiful story out of them.

That happened while I was ministering at the International Church of Las Vegas. The pastors there, Paul and Denise Goullet, are dear to us and had invited me to minister at their church. I had yet to hear God's voice that night (I hate to teach on a subject and then not demonstrate or activate it), however during the amazing worship I began to get a few impressions and word clues and wrote them down.

One of my favorite stories from that night involved a family from the church. When I pointed to them, addressing one family member by name, I repeated a date, which ended up being that person's birth date. Then I said another first and last name. At once, their closest friends gasped. They told me it was the name of their cousin's murderer. This man had obviously caused much brokenness in the family. Then I gave them some information that only the family knew and understood.

"Give this young man and the pain he has caused to God," I said.

"Let God deal with him, and He will. He is taking this pain from you if you give it to Him."

I've scaled down this story to leave out some of the private details, but the heart of my time with this family, especially this young family member, reinforces the redemptive nature of our God. This young girl had been dealing with so much and was visibly overwhelmed by her cousin's killing. She had no real resolution. Now, she finally had hope that God had seen the situation and would deal with it. She could trust God to wield justice. Finally, this young girl felt some real release.

In his gospel, John shares the words of Jesus, reminding us of His power and promise to make things right in a broken world:

I have said these things to you, that in me you may have peace. In the world you will have tribulation. But take heart; I have overcome the world (John 16:33, ESV).

I love that Jesus shares His heart here. To those who will listen and who will trust in His voice, He promises to create a place of peace, even during times of drama and hurt. His truth offers us confidence in the fact that God is with us. We can overcome because He has overcome. He went to the cross and was raised up from death so that He already has the victory over anything we face. When you know what's in His heart, you don't have to fear what is in another's heart or the trials of this world. When you know God's heart and mind, you can overcome anything in this world.

REVELATION HELPS US SEE GOD'S THOUGHTS AND ORIGINAL PLANS

In the 1980s, some of my dear friends, Che and Sue Ahn, went to a meeting searching for encouragement. As pastors of a small church, they were hungry to know what God wanted from them. Their church had been experiencing an outpouring of God but also had the usual trials that go along with fruitful ministry activity.

The speaker at the meeting was a prominent traveling minister who focused on spiritual gifts. He was receiving such clear and accurate revelation that leaders across diverse spheres of influence sought him out to hear what God might be saying to them. Che and Sue had been around these kinds of prophetic personalities before, but how specific this man was in his words of knowledge really caught their attention. Throughout the night, they were stunned as this man prophesied over people in such specific ways that just said, "This is for you." Everyone who was prophesied over felt the miracle of God's manifest presence. God was in the room, and He cared!

Then this minister asked the crowd, "Is there a Che and Sue here?" My friends were shocked! No one knew they would be there. He actually knew their names by a word of knowledge and told them that God was with them. They couldn't believe he knew their names! Che is a Korean name—not at all a common name in the relatively dominant Caucasian crowd. There was no way this minister could have known them or even known they would be there. His question sent a spiritual wave of God's presence through Che and Sue: God knew them by name.

It was what they so desperately needed to hear. My friends were in an uncertain season of life and ministry and knowing that God was with them—that He really knew them—gave them necessary assurance. I love that they were pastors and needed a word from God! Their desperate seeking is inspiring for all of us who want to know that God is with us.

That little endorsement—the fact that God knew their names— carried Che and Sue through years of pioneering a church movement that now has more than twenty-thousand affiliated churches. Che related their story to me, stressing the powerful impact of simple, revelatory information on the heart of someone who loves God. Feeling assured that God knew him by name, throughout the years of flourishing ministry, Che pondered these things in his heart. No matter how mature we are or how deep our relationship with God is, we can always use another "I love you forever!" moment.

Revelation helps us to see God's original thoughts and plans for humanity, restoring us to our full destiny of connection to our Creator and Savior—a connection that brings everlasting life. Words of knowledge help us know that we're part of God's original plan and thoughts and that He cares deeply about every aspect of our lives. None of us are mistakes. God has pre-thought and planned all of us in intricate detail. No matter what we've done to sabotage our lives or what the enemy has done to try and destroy God's plan before we were saved, God sent Jesus to restore us to that original state of His purpose for us.

Words of knowledge are one of the fastest ways to build connection to the heart and mind of God. When you know *you* are what God has on His mind, like my friends Che and Sue experienced, that kind of assurance will change you forever!

THE INFORMATION AGE

We live in an Information Age, where information is king. In some ways, information is easy to come by, but in other ways it's so valuable that companies spend billions a year gathering it for all kinds of reasons. Demographics, security, marketing, education—information fuels and advances so many areas of our lives.

In fact, that's what marketing is. Businessdictionary.com tells us marketing is based on thinking about the business in terms of customer needs and their satisfaction.[1] If you have a product to bring to market, information will play a key role in reaching the consumers who might be interested in buying it. You'll need to know everything about the people who are likely to use it, how they'll use it, and when they'll use it. For example, a politician who's trying to find her place in government will need to know her party and the other parties involved

---

[1] *www.businessdictionary.com* ||Definition of Marketing

in her system to represent the current issues in relevant ways. Likewise, a pastor will have to understand the city or region he's pastoring, not just his local congregation.

Across all humanity, we continue to realize that the more information we have, the more successful we are in any field. The more knowledge we have of the people directly and indirectly involved with our field, the more influential we will be. The more we know others, the more impact we'll have. Knowledge is key.

That said, have you noticed that people have begun to substitute information and knowledge for relationships? Some churches have even followed the way of businesses and politicians. They are managed through structures or organizations more than connections and a family culture. Instead of seeking to have a deep connection with their people, they seek knowledge *about* them to fill a need. Community needs are being met, but sometimes deeper issues are left untouched and neglected.

Focusing on meeting community needs more than facilitating spiritual transformation sets us up for a performance mentality. People get into deep performance mode because they don't want to be vulnerable in ways that might affect the church's ability to meet needs. When churches focus on spiritual transformation, they allow people to share their weaknesses or vulnerabilities. As a result, the whole community will grow from it.

At times, the prophetic gifts in today's church have mimicked this performance mentality. We've injected these spiritual words into organizations and people in ways that bring about performance goals. Telling people what they should do or giving directions that don't necessarily help them to be more Christlike, or lead them to a spiritual transformation, can create a *purpose driven-ness*. This sometimes emerges out of a lack of identity. The prophetic is so beautiful because it isn't meant to focus on knowledge alone. Instead, through words of knowledge, we give people a picture of who they can be, or what they can achieve, through their relationship with Christ. We go way beyond just giving them information.

WORDS OF KNOWLEDGE HELP BREAK US OUT OF PERFORMANCE MODE

I believe God is releasing words of knowledge in this generation as a primary form of manifesting the rest of His prophetic gifts. He wants to break through the manipulative ways in which we use natural and spiritual information to get ahead, to help us get out of a performance mentality. In other words, God doesn't just want to tell us what to do or fill us with knowledge alone. He wants His words to communicate His love and devotion toward us: *I have loved you with an everlasting love. I know your name and you are mine. I have plans for you forever, not just in this lifetime. There is nothing you can do to earn my love.*

In a very real sense, God is using information—in a way the world doesn't always choose—to validate our identity and His love for us.

The prophetic gifts are supposed to first display love, acceptance, mercy, compassion, and the nature of God to whoever is receiving the prophecy. Instead, for years, people have misused or mishandled the prophetic gifts as a means of finding their identity through their "performance."

We have all heard about or witnessed the misuse of the prophetic gifts—everything from, "God will judge you if you don't do such and such" to, "Your destiny is to be in this performance ministry title or business title," to, "You are called to give up everything and go to the nations." These words may not sound inherently bad (I've shared the second two examples in different ways with people). But when they don't come from, or to, a person who operates out of love for people or who nurtures a relationship with God above their mission in life, they become driving words that actually play into our societal identity issues.

God doesn't just want to disseminate information so that we have new knowledge to assimilate into a life of performance. The primary focus of revelation isn't about giving us knowledge so that we can be wiser in how we maneuver through life (although this does happen as a secondary effect). God gives us revelation to reveal who He is and who we are to Him. In the same way, the Father sent Jesus to the world to reveal a redemptive picture and restore our relationship with Him. The prophetic gifts reveal God's nature, His heart, and our eternal destiny with Him. Giving or receiving words of knowledge is much more than an incentive or motivator for how we live our lives; this gift puts God at the center of our lives, as He becomes our main desire and focus.

WORDS OF KNOWLEDGE REVEAL THE MIND OF A LOVING GOD

I have pursued prophetic gifts for my whole life, especially to prophesy over others. This has marked my teaching and missions ministry. A few years back, I started to get words of knowledge that led to receiving other words. I would begin with a combination of a few details that usually applied very specifically to someone I had no idea would be there.

When I gave people prophetic words or ministered to them one on one, I noticed a pattern of how God's love was revealed right away.

First, I would hear God give me dates, mostly the birthdates of the people I was praying for. I asked everyone if a certain date meant something to them and so many times it was their birthday. I love this! Millions of years before we were born (or even forever before we were born since God is timeless), God knew He was going to create us. Through birthdates, He acknowledges how planned and well thought out we were. Every person loves to hear, "Happy Birthday! I celebrate your life."

A few years ago, my family took me on an adult trip to celebrate my birthday and, of all places, we went to Disneyland. It was for my 38th birthday. Anyone who's been to Disneyland for their birthday probably knows to go to guest services to get a shiny, personalized "Happy Birthday" button to wear all day. But I was surprisingly overwhelmed to get this birthday button with my name on it.

Everywhere I went, every cast member (that's what Disney calls all its employees) I saw gave me a big smile and said, "Happy Birthday!" All day long, I felt like a kid who'd just found Davy Jones's locker full of buried treasure. It was an incredible lesson. These birthday greetings said something way beyond, "Happy Birthday!" They also said, "I see you! Your life matters!" My birth was not random. The world around me acknowledged that this planned event was important. Surprisingly, my love language (what makes you feel loved) is not "words of affirmation." However, this day at Disneyland chock full of "Happy Birthday!" greetings encouraged me when I thought of God's love for me in light of these two words.

That's how a word of knowledge is supposed to make you feel: *Your life has meaning. You are someone's favorite. You have a God who wants to spend forever with you. You are loved. And on top of that, you were born for a reason. You are celebrated. You can do what you were born to do. Your nature and personhood are worthy of connection. Your family is better because you're alive. Because you exist, the world is impacted and changed.*

I still remember one of the meetings I was invited to where the beauty of a name and a birthday changed a young girl's life. My worship-leader friend Cody and I were ministering over the crowd together. At one point, I heard a date connected to a name: "Barbara." When I asked if there was a Barbara with that birthdate, a teenage girl in the crowd began to cry hysterically. As I gave her the word God had for her, this girl's friends began to pray for her. Later, Barbara came up to me and told me she had been asking God for a year, "Does my being born have any significance? Can my life make a difference for anyone on Earth? Do I even matter, or am I just another person You created?" When I called her out by her name and birthday, this young teen's suicidal thoughts left her—she felt heard by the God of all the universe. Her life had incredible significance. And now she knew it.

After birthdays, I began to also hear the dates of anniversaries. I remember the third time this happened in a specific way. I asked a couple if June 17 meant anything to them. Turns out, it was their wedding anniversary. I said to them, "God loves your marriage so much, and He picked you for each other." They both burst into tears. They told me they were at such a hard place in their marriage. Words of knowledge healed years of disconnect by giving this couple so much hope. Jesus loved their marriage. It could be a good one again!

Another time, I asked a man in front of the whole church if a certain date meant something to him.

"Not specifically," he said.

I thought I'd missed it until he and his wife came back the next day to tell me it was the date of their anniversary. She couldn't be in the meeting but was watching online and was horrified that he had forgotten it. Maybe the whole point of this word was to help him forever remember their anniversary. (I'm so glad that wasn't me! I still know the day I married Cherie.)

An anniversary date became extremely significant at The Call Azusa (the historic event I talked about in Chapter 1). I shared the names and anniversary date of a couple and asked the crowd if there was anyone there with those names and anniversary date. The husband, Montell, was there, but his wife was not.

"You made the best choice of your lives that day!" I told him.

What I didn't know was that this couple had all but given up on their marriage. That week, they had planned to officially separate.

Through words of knowledge spoken out in an arena filled with people, I described how the couple met and dated, and how God was in their marriage. I had no idea that this word from God would soak up the pain of years of neglect and discord. The whole crowd began to celebrate their marriage and how the couple met.

After the event, this lovely couple released a response video to that word they had received in front of millions watching on TV. Their marriage was worth it! They would fight for it.

After birthdays and anniversary dates, street addresses started to come to me. The first time I heard a street address, I heard, "Shady

Pine Drive." I was in a public meeting and asked, "Does anyone live at Shady Pine Drive?" A woman screamed. She had lived isolated from everyone. After her husband died, she had felt so alone and had been praying and asking God, "Do You see me? Do You even know where I live?" And here I come, prophesying and shouting out the name of her street. I could have said nothing else, and she would have walked away assured that God knew her and had answered her sadness with hope.

Another time, I publicly prayed for a family at a church meeting. I started off by giving directions to their house. I told them where to turn and what streets they were turning on to get to their house.

"That is it," they told me.

Then I said their address and told them that God was going to meet with them there. They were leaders in this church and for decades had hosted groups and families in their home. They were looking so forward to learning what the next season of their lives and ministry would look like. God knew where they lived, which gave them huge anticipation about what He would do. They knew it would be something even more special than what they had already experienced. I've learned that when I receive revelation about a street address, people feel valued by God. He knows where they live.

There have been many other types of words, including words about finances, extended family, and ministry, but with an emphasis on people feeling known by God.

One night after a meeting, God gave me a word for a couple sitting behind us in, of all places, a local diner. I turned around and began to play with their two-year-old who couldn't keep her eyes off of us. I built a rapport with the couple, and they asked what I was doing in town. They had heard I was visiting. I told them I was ministering at a local church and asked if there was anything I could pray for in their lives.

"Yeah, that we win the lottery!" the wife said.

"Yeah," I laughed, "Powerball nights trigger the biggest prayer meetings in America—nationwide prayer!"

I had no idea this couple was living through a difficult financial recession. Then I had a spiritual experience. I could hear a long number.

"Does this number mean anything to you?" I asked.

They both looked very shocked. I had just recited their Bank of America account number. I could tell they were afraid and, at first, a little weirded out.

"God knows your bank account number," I said. "Isn't that amazing?"

"It's empty though," the woman said.

"God showed me this number, which means He is thinking about your finances more than you are and has financial hope for you! It won't be empty for long if the God of all the universe knows about it!"

They both sat wide-eyed! The husband admitted he didn't really believe in God, but our conversation had changed everything. I also insisted on paying their check, which they tried to refuse.

"What kind of new friend would I be if I knew your financial situation, even your bank info, and didn't help you out?" I said. "I'll either pay now or deposit it to your bank! Take it in the spirit of friendship!"

The friends I was with also gave this couple some money and instead of it feeling like weird charity, it felt like we were helping family.

That whole experience must have been so crazy for them!

Here's this mysterious man from Los Angeles who knew their bank account number and had a message for them that God knew their need and wanted to fill it.

I could go on and on sharing stories of how God has used me to share a poignant date or detail in the life of a person. The principle of words of knowledge is this: *God is thinking about us and knows us and loves us!*

If I hear a word of knowledge and speak a spouse's name, people tend to feel like they married the right person and that God is in their relationship. If He reveals the name of their business, people value their work more. If I share the name of the college where they graduated, people find assurance that they are on track for their education. The list goes on.

Words of knowledge help give us a sense that God is in all of the normal and sometimes mundane places in life—until He shows up. Then the everyday places become extraordinary and important.

Once you start to grow in a life of words of knowledge, you begin to hear God's thoughts about humanity. This goes much deeper than just knowing basic information about people. You start to know God in the way He wants to be known. You start to give wisdom, revelation, insight, and counsel in a way that only a master strategist or counselor could. The endgame of getting words of knowledge is not just giving people special words. What if God could trust us to counsel nations? What if we knew His heart about things that most of humanity is dying to know?

Prophetic gifts aren't words that tickle ears or parlor tricks for unsuspecting people. They are fellowship with the God who transforms us and is transforming the world (more on that in future chapters)!

THE BLACK AND WHITENESS OF WORDS OF KNOWLEDGE

When someone experiences a healing miracle, the moment is in real time. The person receiving the miracle knows he is stronger so God must be real. A word of knowledge has the same kind of miraculous tendency. It is God showing up right now with information you couldn't have known or heard without a supernatural connection to God.

Unless you have your goal set right, those black-and-white moments can create anxiety in our pursuit of miracles and words of knowledge. By the way, in case you're wondering, the goal is, and always should be, love. If you pray for a healing miracle for a broken leg, and it remains broken, have you wasted your time? No! We first show love and value for the person we're praying for. In doing so, we give God an opportunity to move, heal, and even bring a miracle. In the same way, the gift of words of knowledge is worth practicing. Regardless of the outcome, this prophetic gift comes from a place of trying to access the heart of God. Practicing it is always a worthy effort.

Other types of revelatory gifts, like prophecy, council, words of wisdom, and tongues might take time to play out and need to be interpreted and pondered. But the gift of words of knowledge comes with an instantaneous revelation of, "God is here *right now*." The immediacy of the moment can create such an awe of who God is. Scripture describes this awe as the fear of the Lord. The instant understanding that God is with us and that He cares causes us to desire to be closer to Him and protect our connection with Him.

The black and whiteness of words of knowledge also comes into play when the information we give someone is incorrect. If you ask someone if their name is Barbara and it's LaShawndra, she'll think you haven't heard from God. These absolutes make practicing this a high-risk gift. The stakes sometimes feel too overwhelming. It's one of the reasons why people in the body of Christ have not run after this gift. As we talked about earlier in this chapter, we've wrapped up too much self-imposed "performance" into the revelation gifts.

Many of us have been taught that people who are gifted in the prophetic are born with it and are infallible. This fallacy creates such a wrong responsibility for the people who practice this gift, as well as for those who are brought up to believe it. This untruth deflates the faith of everyday Christians and deters them from pursuing and practicing the prophetic gifts.

PRESSING PAST THE PAIN

I rarely have any regrets now, but part of the pain of maturing comes when you don't know how to be you and to let God be God. I look back and can see times when my insecurity has caused me to fumble opportunities. Part of maturing is feeling full enjoyment when God provides you with opportunities. When you know how to get out of the way and yield, you get to just glory in what God has done through you.

I remember walking through our local mall and seeing a woman from another country working hard to get her two toddlers and stroller up the escalator. It was obvious that the rude Americans trying to get by her were judging her for choosing to take the escalator instead of trying to find an elevator (in America, we don't bring strollers up escalators because they might eat our children). The air was filled with tension as the people waited impatiently behind her, irritated over this small act of a mom trying to get to the next level of the mall. One man even pushed past her, completely ignoring her plight and knocking a bag out of her hand.

I ran over and grabbed the stroller and her bag while she managed the kids. By the time we got up the escalator, her frustration had almost brought her to tears. I could tell this small incident probably played into some very real-life circumstances her family was going through. She thanked me over and over. I was about to walk away, but as I said goodbye to her cute little crew, I felt heaven pull on my heart to take a risk.

"Can I ask you something?" I said. "I'm having a spiritual moment and wanted to know if you're moving soon because of your husband's job?"

She looked shocked. "Yes!" she responded. Without questioning the spirituality of my moment or that I even had one, she opened her heart (which seems to be the common response when this happens) and began to tell me their whole story. Her husband had been estranged from his family and family business, but his stepfather was dying, so his brother had reclaimed the business. He wanted to share it with his brother. They were moving to Texas to start a new life but she was feeling nervous about the move.

"Being from Ukraine, I have never been to Texas," she said with an amazing Eastern European accent.

"Is your husband's name Steve?" I asked. She said no.

At this point, I could have stopped there, let my insecurities take over, forgotten that this was not about me but what God wanted to say to her, and ruined the moment. But I felt an inner prompting: *Stay engaged with her, Shawn, don't worry about you.*

So I went for broke.

"I'm a Christian, and I feel like God is showing me that He's restoring your husband's family and the family business to give your kids the legacy that is their birthright. This move to Texas is from Him!"

She had tears in her eyes. It seemed as if something inside her shifted and lifted the pressure and fear. She literally fell into me with a hug.

"You are not only going to be okay," I continued, "but God is moving in this and wants to help you in all of it. He is good."

She looked at me and replied, "I have never known God could speak or be like this."

Over the next twenty minutes, two miracles happened. I shared the gospel with her, and she asked Jesus to show her who He was. The second was subtler, but as a parent, I knew God had intervened. Her toddler kids stayed completely absorbed with each other and at peace, giving her the opportunity to ask questions and listen, uninterrupted (any parent knows that's a true miracle). Later, I found out her husband already knew Jesus but hadn't really connected to his faith in decades. That changed as they moved back into their God-sent promised land.

In hindsight, I realize how much this story taught me. Of all the things that I spoke to her about, I personally felt the strongest revelation connection about her husband's name. I really felt his name was Steve. There was no Steve. Those moments can be jarring.

I have learned to not super-spiritualize everything, and that has freed me from getting stuck in the details and trying to find meaning or validation for every piece of revelation I might go after. If you want to grow in this gift of words of knowledge, you must move past whatever isn't working and reevaluate.

You also must release any pride that comes from being "right." When it comes to revelation gifts, the need for validation or even the need to be right is a spiritual growth killer. As humans, pride isn't unique. But I have honestly seen so many people still stuck in this trap. By getting stuck on their own invalidated revelation, they ruin perfectly good moments they initiate with prophetic words.

Many just run over the people who can't corroborate their revelations. I've seen people share spiritual words and act like the person they're talking with is the one in the wrong ("when they're more spiritual or have time to pray, it will all work out"). It is such a presumptuous, and yet, prevalent, attitude that emerges when insecurities often accompany these prophetic gifts.

Though I felt so strongly about the name, there really wasn't a Steve. I have talked to this woman since that first day, and the name "Steve" has never come up. It was nothing. Because I focused on the words that *were* connecting, she never even noticed this incorrect detail. She just felt so known by Jesus and so loved by God during a time when she desperately needed security and stability. Through revelation, *God* comforted her that day when she was standing in a mall and everything felt out of control.

I'm so happy that God has worked with me to show me that my identity comes through *Him* as His son and heir, not His *gift*. And I'm thankful I didn't let my insecurities ruin her moment. Resolve to press past these insecurities and any performance issues. I believe you'll find great enjoyment in the revelatory journey.

WHY LOVE IS MORE IMPORTANT THAN ACCURACY

Because revelatory ministry is developed differently in the New Testament than in the Old Testament, we know the prophetic gifts are no longer about just information given to people, but rather expressing God's love to the world around us. In the Old Testament, a few leaders led the many with words they had to steward with a different type of faith. As a way to lead His people into His will and desire, God gave priests, judges, prophets and kings instructions, directions and decrees that were all about carrying out His infallible will. Repeatedly, the Old Testament shows us that when God's people didn't listen to their leaders and obey His word, they directly or indirectly suffered the consequences of their rebellion. And if a prophet dared to speak for himself or even lied, he could be (and usually would be), stoned for his disobedience.

The leaders we read about in the Old Testament didn't hear God in a still, small voice. For the most part, His voice came as a clear instruction or as complete messages. I'd guess that most of the leaders we read about didn't wonder, *Is that the voice of God?* His voice and His message were usually loud and clear. From His call to Abram to leave the land of his forefathers to His call to Moses to lead His people out of Egypt, God spoke very clearly to His people. Of course, in the Old Testament God's people didn't share in the full mind of Christ through the Holy Spirit's indwelling. Instead, they were subject to God "hovering" over them, "covering" them and "overshadowing" them—words used throughout the Old Testament to describe God's interaction with His people before Christ came down.

Before Jesus, the whole model of God's relationship with His people was obedience. It was proof of someone's devotion to his Lord and is still such a great example to us today. Throughout Scripture, we see the nation of Israel justified by their leader's obedience or damned by their turning away from God.

So when Jesus broke through God's four-hundred-year silence (the amount of time between Malachi and Matthew, where God did not speak to the people), the model for how He spoke to His people changed. In his Gospel, John shares Jesus' words: "To him the gate-keeper opens. The sheep hear his voice, and he calls his own sheep by name and leads them out" (John 10:3, ESV).

In other words, Jesus shares how He will talk to us. He is a good-natured shepherd who leads us to green pastures and says, "My sheep know My voice."

After his resurrection in the upper room, Christ promised His disciples that the Holy Spirit would be sent to tell them what was in the Father's heart. Consider Jesus' words and His description of the Holy Spirit's role in our lives:

I have much more to say to you, more than you can now bear. But when he, the Spirit of truth, comes, he will guide you into all the truth. He will not speak on his own; he will speak only what he hears, and he will tell you what is yet to come. He will glorify me because it is from me that he will receive what he will make known to you. All that belongs to the Father is mine. That is why I said the Spirit will receive from me what he will make known to you (John 16:12-15).

Then, in the early church, we see examples of how the believers prophesied from the heart of God. Paul even does us a favor and lists the spiritual gifts that are given to build up the body. This, though, is also in context of a new, ground-breaking theme. Now, because of Christ's sacrifice and atonement for our sins, we are no longer separate from God, relying on prophets to share His mind and heart. I get excited every time I think of this new paradigm. Now we are *each* a priest— able, justified and accountable to how we hear from God. Someone else's revelation can only complement what we're personally hearing from our Creator. Revelation is not supposed to substitute for our own responsibility to seek and obey His voice in our lives.

While people in the Old Testament were subject to the authority of their leaders, who heard from God through revelations, throughout the New Testament we see that revelatory gifts take a backseat to this personal authority. These gifts, Paul says, are now for encouragement, comfort, direction, edification, exhortation and bringing us into the mind of God, so that we can make prudent decisions and connect to the world around us with God's desires merged with our own.

In the New Covenant, we are accountable to God for what we hear from Him and the council He puts around us. We are no longer bound to listen to someone else's spiritual agenda as a primary message for our lives. We don't have to be justified by a priest or a leader in our faith.

I could almost promise that when you get to heaven no one will call you by name and say, "You should have followed your pastor more." If we're even asked questions, I think we'll hear questions similar to the ones Jesus asked His disciples: "Did you learn how to love Me and know Me? Did you live a life surrendered to My love?" The only one we have been called to follow is the One who gave Himself that we may live an abundant life on Earth (see John 10:10) and in eternity with Him (see John 3:16). No one is a mediator between you and God the Father except Jesus. People who might have been your source for affirmation in God become secondary to God Himself. This is a great thing!

Let's go back to John, this time as an aged church leader, writing to people who struggled with discouragement due to the presence of false teachers: "You don't need anyone to teach you," he writes, "but you have an anointing that will teach you" (1 John 2:20). In other words, the Holy Spirit is here to guide you into being the fully empowered version of who you are called to be. This "final" or "eternal" version of yourself is in God's mind all of the time. This is how He sees you and how He wants the world to treat you.

As it says in The Message version in Romans 2:2, "Unlike the culture around you, always dragging you down to its level of immaturity, God brings the best out of you, develops well-formed maturity in you." (Romans 8:29 The Message).

God knew what He was doing from the very beginning. He decided from the outset to shape the lives of those who love Him along the same lines as the life of his Son. The Son stands first in the line of humanity He restored. We can see the original and intended shape of our lives in Him.

John tells us that no one is responsible for us hearing God. That responsibility lies solely with us. No one is your ultimate leader, except Jesus. You can hear God and discern His heart.

What does that mean for you and me as we grow in sharing words of knowledge? The biggest thing is that the pressure for us to be "right" is gone.

This now rearranges the priorities of the purpose of revelation. I can't be stoned for getting information wrong, but if, for example, I try to prophesy over someone and I'm wrong about it and then don't take responsibility for being wrong, I sure can violate a relationship. In other words, my primary goal of pursuing revelation is to try and connect God's heart of love to someone. As I am doing that, the goal isn't to deliver the information in the most correct way. It is to get to know God's heart for the person and to speak to them with that value, treating them with that heart. Sometimes I might not have a full revelation to give, or I might act on something that isn't clear or even correct. But if my goal is to love the person in Jesus, then the actual prophecy is secondary to the goal of loving and connecting.

If I'm wrong with a word of knowledge, I can just move on, do some course correction, or even stop with that particular interaction. Being wrong doesn't disqualify or negate the accurate things I've said. It just means I'm still learning how to connect to and translate God.

In the New Testament, we see the apostle Paul engaging the church with relational and social responsibility. I talk about this in my books *Translating God* and the *Translating God Workbook*. I encourage you to read these to learn more about personal accountability and tracking words. In both of these books, I center on the fact that because Jesus is training us in the culture of His heart and mind, most of the time we're not directly hearing from Him, because He wants us to carry the Kingdom culture of *who* He is, not just serve *what* He is. In other words, Jesus rarely spoke directly to the crowds. Instead, He told stories that helped people understand what it looked like to relate to God, His kingdom, and the world around them. Through parables, stories, and mysteries, He imparted the love of His Father in ways that enabled people to know what He was truly like. He longed to share *Himself* with everyone, not just His works.

That's why there's so much beauty in a life filled with words of knowledge. Nothing is more beautiful than knowing Jesus. Through words of knowledge, we meet our Savior in a real way, that not only goes beyond our imagination, but also reveals an intimate relationship that says, "I know you. There's something more."

3

THE GROWTH PROCESS, TOOLS TO HELP

A s I've said before, the reason I'm writing this book and sharing my experiences with you is to show you in a very real way that you can grow in this gift. You can know God's secrets— His heart and His mind. Part of this happens through practice. Part of it happens through growing in your dependence on His heart and nature, through a real connection to Him. To understand how to grow, you need to use a biblical framework and some modern applications of this amazing gift.

You also need to know about some of the obstacles you'll encounter, as well as how to jump into this kind of faith and connect to a lifestyle of words of knowledge.

THE MOST IMMEDIATE RISK

Growing in the gift of words of knowledge is no more challenging than pursuing any of the revelatory gifts. It's just more cut and dry, and that requires us to take more risks. For example, you can't say to someone, "I feel like your birthdate is in May," without it being absolutely right or wrong.

Unfortunately, absolute statements keep many people off the growth track of high faith and high risk. If you think about it, for most people the risk factor makes prophesying over someone relatively easy compared to sharing words of knowledge. While prophecy can feel powerful in the moment, it comes with delayed risk. You're not immediately on the hook for the outcome.

Very few people ever check back in with those they prophesy over to track their words, often resulting in stunted spiritual growth and no sense of responsibility. Without a tracking process in place, they have no way to evaluate themselves. But when words of knowledge are incorrect, the responsibility is instant, requiring us to do unexpected and immediate self-evaluation.

So how can you practice words of knowledge and take great faith risks? Simply put, you'll need to be open to failure. As I shared in the last chapter, I've sometimes given what I thought were words of knowledge that were just plain wrong, leaving no room for interpretation. But the key thing is I still met my personal ministry goal of loving the person and also experienced great fruit from the interaction.

Then there are the people who can't relate to what I'm sharing and look at me like I'm crazy or, worse, deceptive. Instead of writhing in the sting of rejection, I've learned to just stay in a place of confidence in Jesus. One of my favorite scriptures for all growth pursuits in God is 1 Peter 4:8: "Love covers a multitude of failures!" I love how *The Message* says it: "Most of all, love each other as if your life depended on it. Love makes up for practically anything."

The beautiful thing about *agape* love is that it gives us permission to try and to grow. In anything in life, especially in those areas we're trying to grow or improve in, we'll contend with performance issues. Because we need divine inspiration to even participate with the prophetic gifts, we amplify these gifts when we use them to share words of knowledge or prophesy. Think about it. So much is at stake when you use the words "God told me," or "This is God!" We need to change the rules of engagement so that everything doesn't come with such high stakes!

In my own ministry, I have lowered the stakes by using language and communication in a different way. I ask questions and leverage more of a relational language for communicating words of knowledge or prophecy. The majority of models of prophecy have someone saying a run-on sentence to someone they've just met—a personal message he or she says originates with God. There is little to no interaction, no fact finding, no rapport building, and no feedback. If we want to grow and change the stakes, we have to change this prevailing model. Here's an undeniable truth: If God is the most relational being in the universe, then as people created in His image we're allowed to also be people who relate to others.

Using soft language and then asking questions is important. For example, the statement "I feel like March might be an important month for you. Is there anything happening in March?" gives a person time to interact with you and be part of the process. If her birthday's in March, she'll feel just as special as if you steamrolled her, shouting, "YOUR BIRTHDAY IS IN MARCH, AND GOD WANTS TO TELL YOU SOMETHING!"

When we use a lot of hyper-spiritual prophetic language, we run the risk of exaggerating, or not truly connecting to the heart of the word that God has for someone. Just as we have more emotional intelligence in this generation than at any other time in history, we need more spiritual intelligence to help us discern how our models are working or failing.

I realize that when we change some of the models that are out there, we risk coming across as not as confident or maybe softer than people want to be. But the risk/reward ratio is there. If we risk for relationships, then we'll change our delivery. If we risk for information gathering, then we'll likely run right over the relationship.

I also believe that people in this generation want to feel like they're part of a conversation. Across so many spheres (education, leadership development, business, and government), the communication models are changing to appeal to emerging generations. The prophetic sphere is inherently relational, so there's no reason not to initiate a conversational model as well.

YOUR INTERNAL RATING SYSTEM

We all have many ways we hear from God: Impressions, internal words, external audible words, dreams, visions, etc. (see the Appendix for detailed definitions). We have a responsibility to learn how much risk to take, based on what we're feeling or translating in the revelation we get.

I remember a while back, when one of my friends, who had never heard God's voice before, for a significant decision, decided he had heard from God about his future wife. It didn't hurt that it involved the prettiest girl in our church of 5,000. In a moment of loneliness, my friend said that God had spoken to him that this girl would be his spouse. He felt like God had showed him her favorite thing, which was horses. He had no previous knowledge of this, and when he found out later that she liked horses, he took that as validation.

This guy was 100 percent convinced, with no other confirmation. However, he didn't have a track record for hearing God, a process for holding himself accountable, or even the faith to take risks that were minor before he took a major one.

Needless to say, these nuptials didn't ever happen. Today, they are both married to different people and they never even dated. Back then, he was frustrated with his relationship with God. He just knew he had found "the one." I explained to him that he had to learn how to take risks based on what he was hearing, but also to take things one at a time, in bite-sized pieces. God never tells us to take on a giant without sending us a lion and bear to fight first. As we build history and depth, we begin to know how to make bigger and bigger choices and take risks as we go. I've never watched someone graduate from college who didn't first go through elementary or high school. The same is true in discipleship with Christ. We have educational processes that we shouldn't run past. When we do, we end up feeling incomplete on the other side.

With major decisions, we also can't just jump into a choice with both feet based on a single prophetic word that we haven't spent time processing and praying about. We need to use prophecy as an invitation to fellowship with God's heart, to seek His council, and to do some prayer.

PRACTICE DOESN'T MAKE PERFECT, BUT IT HELPS

Just as a master pianist gets a few notes wrong from time to time, we're going to have experiences that even after much faith, risk, practice, and heart, just don't connect. The good news is that practice makes it so much better. When we practice, we grow in identity, confidence, security, and hope. Practice isn't about getting a lot more opportunities to share your spirituality. It's about learning about your spirituality and connection to God and how to make that palatable to the world around you.

Words of knowledge are going to take tons of practice. Sometimes it seems as if people think I just sovereignly hear God and bypass my twenty-plus years of practice, thinking they can just jump into the gift. *Somehow*, they think, *it will just "work."* In no way am I saying that it will take you twenty-or-so years (thank God!), but you will have to commit to faith and a relationship-building process to grow in and sustain the gift.

Some people also think I was just anointed or imparted to by someone and that I just let their gifting rub off on me and now it's all good and easy. That's not at all the case. I've received some great impartation, but for it to become practical in my life I've had to personally develop and partner with that impartation.

Think of it this way. Can you imagine being someone's parent and buying your daughter a piano and then getting mad at her for not being able to play it the first time she sat down to it? No parent would do that to their child. God is so much kinder than any parent! He allows you to go through a developmental process and even enjoys you as you walk through that process with Him.

However, once you develop in this gift, He enjoys your growth in a different way. Then you're making music for everyone's ears, not just His and yours and the people who love you most. It's not necessarily that He enjoys you more. No parent would ever say, "I hate my baby. I just wish he'd grow up!" Usually, parents joke about wanting their babies back. The reality is that God enjoys your maturity differently, because you were made to live in maturity forever. Infant and childhood stages are for just a minute, but maturity lasts into eternity.

It takes practice, and part of that process is getting to know God and yourself in uncomfortable ways. You'll have to face your insecurities, your lack of identity, your wrong belief systems, and more.

There's nothing like practicing words of knowledge, even if you're feeling like you're playing a crazy guessing game and losing spiritual confidence. For many, that's part of the growth process. I've been there and had to learn what I call the weight of "when it was God and when it was me." In other words, when my words of knowledge connected with someone, I learned what that felt like before, during, and after I shared the words with them. That "weight" helped me when I felt another word, as I could then compare what I was feeling to what I had felt in my spirit the previous time. Sometimes you can only learn that by actually trying it out. When you feel God's weight on your words and they play out with those you're sharing with, you can sense the difference between what is imagination and what is truly spirit.

It's very similar to playing many wrong notes in a song that's one level up from what you've learned. It takes a lot of practice to get the song right, and if you do it from memory instead of reading the notes, you may not be able to apply what you've learned to get better and to play other songs. You may be able to play the music, but understanding it is a different story. God wants to engage you in the process of knowing how to read the music, so to speak—to connect to the relational part of hearing from Him.

The good news is, when you start to make the connections of how words of knowledge work through you, it will carry over into future interactions. Also, you'll often be as blown away and as in awe of God working as the person who's receiving words of knowledge from you. We know that God's thoughts don't originate with us, but words of knowledge connect us to His thoughts so well that we personally grow and learn. I think I enjoy the experience more than the people receiving, and it drives me to keep going. I will tell my friends or wife about what happened and get reenergized to do it all again.

Risk is part of the battle in all of the revelation gifts that have been misunderstood by the church. Learning how to decide on risk based on what you know works (and what doesn't) is an essential principle. Remember that how much you grow in your gift is directly proportionate to how much you practice the gift and the level of risk you take to share it. Of course, if you live in a performance culture, this principle might be foreign to you, as you won't be used to trying things you're not inherently good at doing. But the reality is hardly anyone is inherently good at words of knowledge until they understand their connection to God.

Because I've practiced so many times, I know the weight or measure I can put on believing how accurate a word of knowledge will be. That doesn't mean everything has a heavy weight on it, and by no means am I profound all of the time. It's actually very different from that. For so much of what I'm trying, I can feel a lesser weight, which means I'm still confident but use much softer language or questions.

Then, when I feel a heavier weightiness on how I hear from God, I know I don't have to use qualifiers or soft language in the process.

Also, the environment we're in relationally and socially is important. Am I with believers who understand Christianity and words of knowledge? Then my language is much freer, and the delivery is more comfortable for me. Is it a Christian who has no prophetic experience? Then I try to relate whatever I'm seeing to Scripture or life application, so that he or she can understand God in it. Is it for unbelievers? Then I have to possibly qualify who I am, or that I'm having a spiritual experience and who the source of the experience is.

To give you a real-life view of what I'm talking about, I'll provide some examples:

Normal language for a non-Christian who has not been exposed to words of knowledge and prophecy:

My wife, Cherie, and I were on a phone call with a woman we had just met who had expressed to us that she wanted to explore our spiritual journey. She was of the Baha'i faith and wanted to hear what we believed, which is common and beautiful in the Baha'i faith. (Baha'i's love to listen to others' beliefs.) Cheri and I were sharing back and forth when I heard God for her!

"Farah, can we pray with you?" I asked, knowing she believed in prayer.

"Yes," she said.

After praying for a second, I said, "Farah, I'm having a spiritual feeling about God's heart for you. Can I share it?" Again, she was open to what I had to say.

She had talked about a virtuous life quite a bit in our conversation. I said to her, "In the Bible, God relates virtue to fruit, and we've been talking a lot about virtues. I feel like God is showing me you have a green thumb or are the 'green lady.' Does that mean anything to you?"

Farah laughed and said, "I knew nothing about gardening or farming, yet my husband and I bought a farm with organic fruit. It's doing so well that a magazine ran an article and called me the 'green thumb' lady!"

"Farah," I said, "God knew we would connect and talk about virtue and that He would parallel virtue to your fruit farm. You are a woman of virtue, and God loves you so much [I even told her the farm's street name]. Can we pray that you could connect to God more deeply and that He will give you everything Cherie and I have in our relationship with Jesus?"

She let us pray and prayed along with us.

Even softer language for a non-believer: A friend and I were talking to a friend who was very open to the revelatory gifts but had a huge New Age background. We knew we would alienate her if we started with Scripture or said, "God told me." She was open to having a spiritual encounter with us, so we prayed.

My friend said, "You know I believe in the Creator of the universe. I believe He is showing me that you are so much like Him and that you're extremely creative but you haven't been able to pursue creativity in your occupation due to financial restrictions. I believe He wants to remove those restrictions and give you a creative plan. Can we touch you and ask the Creator to fill you with His plan?"

This woman loved the word my friend gave her and the language he used. She was so touched by the power of God when we touched her that she asked, "What is that?" We got the opportunity to tell her not only what it was but also "who He is." As a result, this personal encounter with His love completely rebranded her idea of God and Jesus.

DISCERNMENT, INTUITION, AND WORDS OF KNOWLEDGE

Most Christians are fully aware of their gift of discernment and rely on it heavily. Do you ever sense when someone is exaggerating? Have you ever heard someone boast about an accomplishment and known they were lying? Have you ever felt like someone wanted to escape a conversation, despite their poker face? Have you ever discerned when someone was struggling with something?

Some of this is human intuition, some of it is people reading, and some is spiritual discernment. All three are valuable skills for a Christian. You may have noticed that this book has a thread running through it that centers on living a connected life. We want to be connected to the world around us and to hear God's voice, avoiding things that might distract or disconnect us.

When you gave your life to Jesus, you were born of the spirit. That means God's Spirit lives in you, and He has ideas and feelings that we tend to sense deep inside. Even if you don't feel intuitive, as a Christian you have a spiritual sensor inside of you that reacts to the world around you. This is where discernment is birthed. We can sense things, especially good and evil.

THE DIFFERENCE BETWEEN A WORD AND DISCERNMENT

We don't have to rely on God to see evil; we are acutely aware of evil all around us. When our spirit is alive in Christ, it's like a magnet, with a positive charge pushing against the negative charge of evil. When we are around evil, it pushes against us. This is one of the ways we discern it. For someone who doesn't know Christ, the whole world can be a volatile minefield. But we have discernment, which helps us sense and navigate the mines. The gift of discernment is a deeply spiritual process and is such a gift from God.

However, discernment is not our final spiritual goal for the prophetic revelation we share with others. Based on our internal, ever-present discernment, we form opinions about politics, relationships, business, other races, etc. Our discernment compels us to make different choices than we would have made before we had tuned into something other than ourselves.

Intuition and discernment can be fully spiritually motivated as well, meaning that discernment is part of us. We live in constant awareness of our gift and use it daily. But sometimes the Holy Spirit intentionally focuses us on something so that we can take it before the Father and get His heart on it.

On the flip side, discernment also causes us to notice things that God might not be focusing us on but that we can still pray about. For example, sometimes when we're personally dealing with a severe hardship or even abuse, we're more discerning of others who are currently going through, or have previously been through, the same thing. Instead of focusing on the negative, we can turn this difficult time into an opportunity for ministry and prayer. We can even train ourselves not to use our discernment to be so focused on noticing what's broken around us.

I know many spiritually sensitive people who have a hard time going to a mall or being in large gatherings because they have allowed their discernment and spiritual senses to dominate their focus—instead of being in the world and not of it (see John 17:14-16). We should be able to disengage from discernable information and conditions.

Here's the hard fact: In training thousands of people in the prophetic, I have had the most difficulty empowering them to take a step past discernment into revelation. This is the number one stumbling block to learning to share what God is showing us, especially among people who feel like their spiritual calling is intercession or anyone whose work centers on inner healing. Because they're so reliant on their discernment, many times discernment becomes the goal of their prayer life or counseling with others, and rightfully so in that context.

But when it comes to prophesying, discernment should always be a tool we leverage to approach our faith in new, maturing ways. It should be a lower priority to us than actually hearing the heart of God.

DISCERNMENT AS A CONVERSATION STARTER WITH GOD

God gives us words of knowledge for encouraging others. It's like all of the prophetic gifts: You see something that God wants to give someone to offer a more personal connection to His Son. He wants people to know that He knows them. If words are shared in a corporate setting, the experience helps people rally around faith for their church, business, city, or people group.

When they share words of knowledge, so many people stop at inner healing or emotional needs. They stop at the spiritual warfare or brokenness they sense. These roadblocks aren't supposed to be the subject of your prophetic words. Sometimes they can help build your compassion and need for boundaries. They can help lead the focus and might even be the entry point for paying attention to what God's saying inside of you. But when God gives you a word for someone, these things aren't supposed to be the things you focus on. We have to show His encouraging heart.

It's important to understand this because if you give what you think are words of knowledge when they're really just coming from your discernment, you won't meet the goal of encouragement. Words of knowledge reveal what God thinks or wants to say about something and can bring a spiritual resolution.

Granted, sometimes we can have a negative subject in a word of knowledge. But it doesn't stay there. When God loves on people through revelatory gifts, they should never leave feeling more exposed than connected. Sometimes, one-on-one breakthrough prayer and even counseling or therapy can set different goals for hearing God's voice. These areas can center more on trying to help someone overcome something and make new choices. This is very different to the more common use of prophetic gifts that we should all strive for—to just give someone the opportunity to be loved on in a supernatural way by God, through knowing His heart.

I've done this one-on-one sharing many times. I remember one fatherless young man in our church. I discerned that no one had talked to him about his sexuality or had sat him down for a man-to-man conversation about managing his sex drive. One night, while a group of us were out late, he opened up to me about some of his struggles, which I'd already discerned. He said he struggled with pornography and even same-sex attraction at times. He was on a journey of sexual identity and self-discovery. Normally, a healthy father figure could bring some solid identity to him. This teen was confused.

Even though I discerned this, he led the conversation. We did an inner healing session, followed by some great times of talking over the next year. God built his confidence in his sexual identity, his physical drive, and his sense of manhood. Where did my discernment come in? It helped me to make choices with him and to be a safe person for him to talk to. It helped him to know that even though I knew what was going on in his life, I didn't judge him. He felt known but not exposed. See the difference in positive versus negative words? I didn't have to start out with words about his sin; he was ready to divulge that. Instead, discernment helped create a conversation that led to him sharing things, so I didn't even have to bring up.

I know this can be confusing in some church cultures, where the goal of personal ministry or discipleship is to overcome sin. Jesus set the goal much higher: to *become* something, not just to *overcome* something. He was always focusing on the disciples—who they *were*, instead of who they *were not*, despite all of the negative things He knew about them. Many times, their negative traits or faults played out right in front of Him, and yet Jesus didn't hold His twelve to these things.

THE WOMAN AT THE WELL

However, be prepared. Negative words might come up as part of a word of knowledge. We have an example in John 4. Jesus walks up to a Samaritan woman and begins talking (never mind that it was illegal for a Jewish man to talk to a woman from Samaria), despite the fact that Jews considered her race unclean. Jesus starts out by telling her that He will drink from her dish, which was unheard of. Then He starts to unravel the Messianic parable.

"Go get your husband," He tells her, "and we can talk." "I have no husband," she replies.

At this point, Jesus gets a word of knowledge that this woman has had five husbands and is now living with another man. But He doesn't condemn or correct her. Instead, He shares with her the way to eternal life. I love that! He didn't receive that word of knowledge to remind her of her shame. We don't have to remind people of their shame. They are already quite aware of it. This word was from a man of love who acknowledged she had never lived a life of love from men. Now, she could have that life of love through Him, the Messiah. He was so kind that He revealed Himself to her even before He shared His true identity with the disciples. Unbelievable!

So there are no hard and fast rules that come with sharing words of knowledge. But there is a protocol of love, sometimes exposing something that someone needs to talk about. For God to reveal private or expository details about someone to you, you'll need to grow in healthy people skills and you'll need a huge heart of love.

USING A NEGATIVE WORD FOR GOOD

A good example: About a year ago, I was at a meeting on the East Coast. Racial tension had been percolating across the country and in some places had come to a boiling point. I had been praying (and still am) that God would bring spiritual resolution.

I asked a woman, "Is there a Daniel in your life? Was he violated by corrupt cops when he was a teenager and then two more times in his twenties when he was wrongfully arrested and even assaulted?"

It was her son.

"Go and tell him that this wasn't God and that it was a misuse of authority. This was an assignment from the enemy to rob Daniel of his authority, because your son is a man of authority. He will hear this word from God and realize who God made him to be. He won't let anyone rob him again!"

She was crying. When she played the word I had for him, the burden of these abusive situations he had been carrying around seemed to just melt away. His trauma was released.

The fruit of this word was so awesome! A few weeks later, Daniel signed up for the police academy! Come on, God! It was his secret dream, and these traumatic experiences had robbed him of it. He couldn't change the past until God showed up and restored him.

Now realize that the word I gave her spoke of negative circumstances. But it was all about what God said to give Daniel hope and life. I love this moment! It showed me that the prophetic gifts can be used to initiate resolutions to some of the deepest issues in the world.

A bad example: Fifteen years ago, I was in a meeting where I did some ministry at the end. Over the microphone, I asked a specific woman if she was having marriage problems. She wasn't, but that didn't keep her from feeling really humiliated. A week later, she wrote me and said several people had come to her, concerned about her marriage. She felt as if she were being labeled.

I learned my lesson and apologized. Even if it's true, exposing something negative like this in a public forum just makes people feel judged and exposed. Ultimately, almost every human being has a sense of self-value and privacy. These types of issues should be addressed in a private setting, in close relationships, and not in a public forum.

GROWING OUR DISCERNMENT

We can grow in discernment based on our life experiences and education. Discernment causes us to be more open to danger and benefit, based on what we've seen God or humanity do. After eating from the tree of knowledge, God hardwired humanity to discern everything. Think about it: After the Garden, everything they ate and drank, and every cave they took shelter in, could kill them. Since then, we've had to rely on discernment for basic survival. We've had to trust our intuition. This wisdom is not always full spirituality though. Often, it leads us to just think about surviving or topics that are good versus bad, instead of thriving and living a full and beautiful heart journey.

Discernment is developed automatically through:

- psychology or counseling
- street smarts
- both negative and positive life experiences
- experiencing brokenness and health in relationships
- teaching, discipling, or coaching a lot of people

In other words, the more you experience your life and humanity through different filters, the more you'll be in tune with certain tools you use to assess people. My mother has done so much inner healing that she can get a feeling about people's emotional or spiritual health right away when praying for them. She has had some counseling training on how to deal with it, which has formed a different slant on her prayer ministry times at churches or in public. She has had to learn that if she's in prophecy or encouragement mode, then she can't rely on her discernment or inner healing gifts as her go-to. If she isn't taking it one step past discernment and hearing the Father's heart, she's not prophesying; she's using discernment to pray through issues with people. Both are valuable, but when we're focusing on how to build revelation, many of us will need to refrain from using our normal discernment and will need to really press in for revelation.

In fact, when you're used to moving in discernment to notice certain themes, you may stop there, because you now know how to read those situations. So, they are obvious to you, even if they're hidden to everyone else. God isn't necessarily asking you to look at those things. He might actually be asking you to look past them to see something totally outside of your viewpoint.

Discernment is so helpful, but people who know me or have heard me minister have heard me say that it's a conversation starter, not a destination. I have to learn to use everything I can from discernment, and not allow it to distract me from focusing on the deeper message coming from God's heart.

Picture yourself praying for a teenage girl and then pretend you have teenagers at home. You can probably feel your own teenagers struggle to find identity in purpose. So you may discern that the teenager is confused about her purpose and future. What if God doesn't want to talk about that at all? What if for this prayer time, He's focused on her family dynamics or friendships, not her future or life purpose?

But because of how you're in tune with your own daughters, you stop at their issues and what you can relate to. God does use what we can relate to all of the time, but then He goes past what we've experienced. Don't be limited by your life experience!

Here's another illustration (can you tell I really want you to get this?): Picture yourself praying for a single person who desperately wants to be married, or a couple wanting a baby. Your compassion moves you because you can discern or feel what's going on in their hearts, especially if you've faced these same issues personally or have walked with someone who has. Your empathy may outweigh what God wants to talk about. What if those desires are their hearts' hot topics, but they're not God's focus for this prayer time with you?

Of course the obvious is true as well—many times our discernment is supposed to lead us. But I want to challenge you to think big about your prophetic prayer assignments with people and make as good and as large of a choice to love as possible.

When you go after the gift of words of knowledge—not being hindered by discernment, but instead experiencing it as a tool toward starting a conversation with the Father—you'll definitely be on track for the authentic and real. There are stumbling blocks to words of knowledge though, and we need to talk about those. On to Chapter 4!

4

IDENTIFYING THE COUNTERFEIT

As I noted in Chapter 2, we live in the Information Age where information about almost anything in the world can be found on the Internet. Do you need to know about Quantum computers? Search the Internet. Apps that digitally track your every move? Our ability to research just about anything also has profound implications on what we can so easily discover about someone else.

With all this access to information at our fingertips, why would I think that God is calling us to focus on restoring our understanding of words of knowledge? Why do we need words of knowledge when we have information sources like the Internet? Because what is revealed through words of knowledge goes way beyond the facts you can potentially research. What God says and does draws a line of authenticity.

Our Father has a story to tell and a connection to make through words of knowledge, which information by itself just can't do. The words that God speaks go deep, expressing a level of authenticity that cannot be duplicated. God is not intimidated by the Information Age, and we shouldn't be either. He can, and will reveal what we need to know when we minister to people. His word is powerful and active; it will not fail us.

Still, there have been many people who, out of deep insecurity and a hunger for significance, have faked their prophetic gifts, especially the gift of words of knowledge. Their ears and egos are tickled when people respond to this powerful gift. They love being the center of people's emotional responses to their ministry, and they get a boost from the financial gifts they receive. So, they manufacture a facsimile of the gift, trying to pass it off as authentic. But the revelation we are going after comes out of His heart and nature, and is the dividing line between what is real and what is fake.

THE REAL EXPOSES THE FAKE

Most ministers, blessed with amazing spiritual gifts, start out in ministry with a real desire to see people transformed. But after years in ministry, the pressure to produce prophetic words and keep their ministries going creates a hamster wheel of performance. I've seen some ministries start to take shortcuts. For others, it's a matter of personal gain and stature. Instead of seeking pure revelation from God, these ministers, overcome with pride and insecurity, choose to fake revelation by searching the Internet. This type of manufactured prophecy has caused some Christians to back away from receiving or giving words of knowledge. This makes me so sad, because hearing from God is supposed to take us *out* of performing in our own strength, not into it!

For every counterfeit prophecy, there is the real deal, and when it comes, it's like a light that casts out darkness. It rebrands whatever came before it with the reality that says, "God is here, He is with me, and He is good."

We cannot allow liars and thieves to set the benchmark for how we minister with good spiritual gifts. Can you imagine finding out that your acclaimed art teacher or favorite artist has never produced an original painting, but instead forged their whole portfolio? Wouldn't it cause you to question the authenticity of the whole art world? Wouldn't you begin to wonder if even Picasso's works were a fraud? What about Michelangelo and the Sistine Chapel? How can you recover your faith in the beauty and originality of fine art after discovering your art teacher's or favorite artist's corrupt lies?

Lies and manipulation, when it comes to the word of knowledge gift, can do the same thing to a person's faith. But we can be healed, and our faith in the power of authentic revelation from God can be restored. When we surround ourselves with things that are beautiful and real, when we pursue the real gifts of God and listen to people who are authentic, we can be healed of unbelief. The fear of being fooled again will dissolve when we encounter the credibility of prophetic culture based in true love.

We have to practice the gifts in the light of love and responsibility. They are powerful tools, but they aren't supposed to be our sole pursuit. We should desire the gift, as they are a manifestation of the love of God being poured out from our lives. Ultimately, they help us to connect with others and lead them to a relationship with Jesus.

WOMAN NAMED JILL

I remember a time when I was ministering at Bethel Church in Redding, California. I was caught up in the Spirit and was taking some huge risks (more about risks in Chapter 6). I prophesied over a woman named Jill, and as I prayed for revelation, I began to receive not only information, but also God's heart for her—His original and connected heart! It's amazing to feel God's intimate love for someone. For me, that level of connection is one of the main benefits of prophetic revelation.

I continued to minister to Jill and began to prophesy very specific things about her mother, Ruth, who had passed away. Ruth was a missionary, and I named countries she had spent time in. Then I named one country, Japan, that she had only spent a little time in but had felt ahuge connection to. I sensed that the Lord would give Ruth the nation of Japan as an inheritance (see Psalm 2:8). So, I told Jill she would carry out her mother's legacy and finish her work. Then the Lord gave me a revelation about medical issues Jill's dad was dealing with, and I felt led to tell her that her dad would be okay, despite the health scare.

I continued, "I see you're adopted from Chicago, but your mom is telling Jesus that she couldn't have loved you any more if you were her own blood. You are her family."

It was one of those amazing, life-changing moments for both of us! Jill received spiritual resolution for what had become deep issues of worth and significance, as well as counsel on what God had planned for her future. For her, this experience was like a kiss from God. He had brought His counsel, and we all felt so deeply impacted and encouraged.

The whole encounter was recorded on video, then posted on the internet, giving a group of Christians who didn't believe in spiritual gifts access to the conversation. They searched Jill's Facebook page trying to discredit me and found some of the information that I had prophesied. They basically dissected the video and claimed that I had access to this information before I ministered to Jill. Even though I had never seen her Facebook page, they were convinced I had and accused me of manipulating the information to get my word to look good or powerful. (This would be so exhausting to do—to try and figure out who's going to be at meetings, research those people, and then give very emotional performances.) But this is what they thought I did.

I understand why these groups would try to "expose" people who prophesy falsely. There has been so much failure and misuse. Also, most people with this expository focus just don't have faith that God can speak to people today, or that He really is just this good and kind. They have probably seen prophetic gifts in operation, and with limited understanding lumped them in with what they label as counterfeit spirituality.

Words of knowledge are an often misunderstood and sometimes disappointing area of pursuit for the church, but I believe God is working through His people to change that. I believe this is an area that God wants to educate and enlighten people in.

I still pray for Jill. She was wonderful about the skeptical inquiry, and without my asking, she even wrote a post about it:

'I AM JILL'

"I am one of those perfect examples of someone you couldn't have researched online. Even if you had somehow looked on my [Facebook] page and seen references to nursing and that my birthday was on September 30, I never referred to my adoption (not because I'm ashamed of it, but it's just never come up, and most of my close friends already know this about me). I've never mentioned that I was born in Chicago (again, not because I was trying to hide it—it has just never come up), and I wasn't even planning to be there at the conference. The morning of the conference, a three-way conversation took place by [private] Facebook message, by email, and through a closed Facebook page that you are not part of, to ultimately get me there. So, there is no chance that you could have known that I was going to be there, because I didn't put it on my Facebook page until after the fact."

"I think my mother's full name is mentioned on the Facebook page in a note that I wrote about her as she was dying (her life story). But you mentioned her middle name to me, not her first name, which I missed the first time around. But if you had taken it from my Facebook page, you would have mentioned her first name. If you had mentioned her first name, it wouldn't have in any way put any question in my mind, but the fact that you used her middle name was actually one of the things that helped me know you were hearing from God and not just reading my Facebook."

"That never even crossed my mind, but when the naysayers started spouting off, that was one thing I was thinking of. If you had been reading the page, you would also have mentioned Persia, where she was born as a missionary kid, as that prominently figured into my note about her on Facebook. And the conversation we had about my ten-year period of difficulty, I've never referred to online. I've had conversations with friends about this, and a conversation with a pastor whom you would have known nothing about. Nor would you have known how I felt about how I would have 'preferred the glorious big things to take place when I was [twenty-five].' You would not have known how my heart carried a big fear about my father dying, as my mother was in process of dying, because I am closest to him, and how he would say to me, 'Well I might die soon so....' or that he had been sick at the two-year anniversary, with the same thing that took my mother out on February 20, or that I cried that day because I thought he was going to die. As I went to get his antibiotic, I went down the street to get the gal who was our caregiver for my mother and asked her to sit with him, because I seriously thought he was going to die, and he was saying he was ready."

"I said none of that online, so there was no way on earth you could have known that ahead of time. For me, because of the conversation I had four days previously with Danny Silk (a pastor at Bethel in Redding), I knew that the word you gave was directly from the Lord to me. I was about to get off track and was very broken up about it, but thought I must have heard God wrong somehow. God was saying, 'Stay the course. I'm bringing the breakthrough. There is so much more.'"

"To those who think that you research everyone and try to put together some big elaborate scheme, I can say with full confidence I know that isn't true and that God Himself was speaking to me through you at just the moment that I needed it. Three of the pastors there at Bethel knew exactly where I was in my journey, and the others all have known me over a twenty-year period. They knew exactly what the word you gave meant and how huge it was for me."

"I've thanked you multiple times before, so this is mostly for those who would question your integrity and character, because I know the truth. Thank you again. Even the leadership didn't know I was going to be at that conference. I haven't been to a conference that is not just for members of Bethel since I was in the School of Ministry, back in 1997."

We don't need to defend each other, but we do need to build this amazing gift of words of knowledge, because we want everything God wants. If you get into debates with unbelieving Christians about this gift, it will almost always go nowhere. Instead, use the energy to pray for them and believe that God will give them a Saul-to-Paul experience in this area. God has even changed much of my own personal beliefs, and some areas where I felt like I was completely serving Him before have become irrelevant compared to what I've since discovered about His love.

It's interesting that in many of my encounters that are scrutinized, the people who are saying I stole that information from somewhere and used it for prophecy are assuming that public information would be enough to speak to the heart of a Christian, especially a mature one. Just tickling someone's ears by mentioning a few details is not enough of an experience for someone really seeking prophetic words from God's heart for the purpose of moving forward in their spiritual life.

COLD READERS/MENTALISTS

One of the most important principles we need to understand is that for every counterfeit spiritual practice, there is probably something very scriptural, something that reveals God's heart. In other words, a lot of counterfeit spiritual practices are based on something completely scriptural, which the devil wants to have power over, so he manufactures his own version. The enemy is smart, yet he can't create. But he can manipulate what God originally designed for how He connects to us. You should never fear something spiritual that is not from God, because, inherently, you're more empowered than the counterfeit.

So many people are unfamiliar with the revelatory gifts. Their limited experience with anything spiritual has come through their unchurched friends or expressions of the supernatural that are not Christ-centered. Their only example of the prophetic may be a psychic, spiritual reader or mystic. Modern media is rampant with the supernatural or paranormal. Think about all of the eerie or creepy television shows, reality series, and movies centered on spirituality and the paranormal. The real version very often gets pigeonholed with the lesser version (aka the counterfeit).

Psychic and medium phenomena, as well as many other types of spiritual pursuit, just don't have Jesus in the middle of them. They are not connected or committed to biblical theology or based on a relationship surrendered to a life of love through Jesus. God wants everyone to encounter Him, to feel how much He loves them. He can use anyone and anything to communicate. He's God! But He consistently uses only those who have a relationship with Jesus and who practice giving revelations about Him.

However, as we model the revelatory gifts in Christianity and share what God is showing us, we may sometimes get accused of being like the world's version. The accusers have never known what it looks like to be connected to God. Sadly, Christians who don't understand the revelatory gifts can sometimes be the worst enemies of revelation, as they're looking for a way to "undescribe" what revelation is supposed to describe—the presence of God manifesting in the here and now out of His great love for us.

SEARCH THE SOURCE

As creations of God, we're intuitive, discerning, and even spiritually aware before we come to Christ. God has unlocked and made available some of His gifts to people, even if they're not living a life connected to Him through Christianity. That's why some people seem to be born with more aptitude toward spiritual gifts, whereas others might be born with more athletic skill or musical talent. We were made to glorify God in different areas and are wired to perform and partner with Him in these specific ways using our gifts. Some people who identify as psychic actually *are* prophetic, but they don't have a relationship with Jesus. So, their revelation doesn't start with or sustain a connection to His heart.

When you're wondering about people's spirituality and expression of supernatural or spiritual gifts, the source is vital. Anyone who pursues spiritual encouragement or aims to encourage others through spiritual reading and does not have a personal relationship with Jesus is probably just a spiritually gifted person. We don't want to seek them out for their revelation gift. At best, we risk misinterpretation by their own very different spiritual expectation or experience; at worst, it can be used by the demonic realm. We really want to hear from Jesus about what He wants. Our purpose in revelation is to serve His agenda, not our own. We fall in love with His desires. Through His mind and will, we feel complete.

Non-Christians who operate in the revelation gifts also do not have relationship boundaries that we, as Christians, have. We know we don't always have to be "on" or spiritually aware of everything around us, but we can entrust ourselves to the living Spirit of God. Instead of having unrestrained discernment and impressions, with no understanding of what we're feeling, we can actually hear when we need to and then be on a need-to-know basis with our gifting. We get to grow in our understanding—not through formula or ritual. Through our personal relationship with God, we learn how to translate what He's saying to us and the world around us.

Think about Daniel. He gave spiritual readings just like the Babylonian astrologers. But Daniel's words of knowledge were grounded in his relationship with God. He was brought to the Saddam Hussein of his day and asked to interpret a dream.

"To King Nebuchadnezzar, Daniel said, 'No wise man, enchanter, magician or diviner can explain to the king the mystery he has asked about, but there is a God in heaven who reveals mysteries'" (Dan. 2: 27-28).

Daniel trusted that God could give revelation to unbelievers, but he knew it was up to the friends of God to properly interpret the heart of His revelation. Out of love, not spiritual superstition, Daniel came to the king to bring revelation with God as the source. God chose his friend to talk to.

WATERING DOWN REVELATION'S PURPOSE

The reality is that when someone pursues revelation for their own purposes and not for a spiritual connection to God, the types of questions they'll ask will be self-absorbed, and will usually indicate a lack of identity. They look for help with lottery numbers and want to know if they should break up with their current boyfriend or girlfriend (two of the top themes of psychics in America: finances and dating). When you're seeking a connected relationship with God and want to hear His voice, you aren't just looking for your needs to be met. Of course, if someone's single, dating will be an important area to them. But it won't be their dominant focus in their relationship with God, as Scripture clearly urges us to live a life that glorifies Jesus. The abundant life we seek happens when we surrender to Him (see John 10:10).

In other words, if you pursue revelation just to get what you need, you're missing the point. But if you're pursuing revelation to know God, and through that relationship you ask about your needs, that's way different. It's a subtle but important difference. One is self-focused; one focuses on relationship. Most negative prophetic ministry encounters happen when the person who's ministering feels like he has to meet someone's needs instead of ministering from God's desire.

THE PURPOSES OF PROPHETIC MINISTRY

When someone practices the prophetic as a gift to just service others' needs, imbalance is usually the result. God never intended for people pursuing prophecy to be well-oiled machines. We pursue hearing God to bring His love to the world. At times, that love creates as many problems as it fixes, because hearing from God is an invitation into a different process. Sometimes we have to fully surrender to walk with Him. This messes with any "normal" we have.

Think of the rich man who came to Jesus and asked, "How can I enter the Kingdom of heaven?" Jesus knew the young man cared more about his lifestyle and the pleasure his wealth brought than anything else. He found his identity in the very thing that destroyed his potential to have a true life. So, Jesus attacked it and said in love, "Sell everything you have and give it to the poor." Jesus' words were an assault on not just the young man's character, but also on his identity. The man walked away confused and discouraged, because he wasn't ready to surrender his life. He wasn't ready for Jesus to mess with his "normal."

For those of us who have been around prophecy, we often think of the prophetic as the "fixer" gift in the church. We hope to hear something that solves our everyday problems and brings an end to our suffering or an injustice. Relief like this can very well happen. After all, God is the giver of great grace that we don't deserve. But His purpose for any revelation is to bring us closer to Him. In prophecy, we see a God fighting for relationship with His children. We see a picture of Jesus who finds His joy in our pursuit of Him and who can't help but speak His thoughts to those who will one day rule His kingdom with Him. Applying these images to the motive behind prophecy makes us seek revelation differently than if it's just a gift with the potential to resolve problems. There is a deeper motivation that centers on a potentially life-changing connection to God.

I remember the first time that I ministered with words of knowledge in a large crowd. It created such a hunger in people to connect to God that they rushed at me. They pushed at me, asking really hard and sad questions: "Should I divorce my husband?", "Where is my 33-year-old son? He's missing. Do you see him?", "Will this cancer kill me?"

I realized that many people in church have a very unsatisfying relationship with God. Even in a lot of Christianity, there is a disconnect between God and man. We don't know or believe that He lives inside us, and that He wants to guide us in real ways and by His love help us navigate our very real problems. In some ways, we don't need a "word" to bring a solution; we need our relationship with God to do that. I do understand the desire when something is missing in our lives to try and get affirmation, but sometimes that can be us just looking for a quick fix instead of a relationship with the God we serve.

On the other hand, it also shows me how quickly we need to grow in these gifts. Can you imagine if we could be a voice that speaks into some of the most critical human dilemmas? What if we *could* help the local police force with missing persons?

I know of a church in Vacaville, California that's beginning to gain more and more trust with their local police force in helping with missing person cases. Or what if we were part of think tanks and were able to really speak into a life-changing product coming to market? I do believe God wants to use His people in that way. Scripture attests to this. Daniel and Joseph were sought after to interpret dreams and give words of knowledge, sometimes by people with the wrong motives. But God used them to not only bless those they were serving, but also to keep His people safe.

PEOPLE JUDGE WHAT THEY DON'T UNDERSTAND

Just like I shared earlier in my story about Jill, you *will* be accused by people in the religious community who don't understand how beautiful hearing God's heart can be. People *will* judge you—based on others' failures, movies that expose false tent revivalists, televangelists who got caught using earpieces, and any other sensational thing that contradicts the awesome gifts of revelation. But if Jesus (who was called the devil Himself by some in the religious community) is our model, and we can relate what the Father is saying to a lost and dying world, the benefit of seeing Jesus get His reward far outweighs others' judgments. You can either come under it, bow to it, or rise above it.

When the real emerges, people forget the lesser example or the fake. Through you, they will feel God's amazing love for them. Instead of worrying about what the enemy is doing and what fakes are doing, just try and be as authentic as possible. You won't avoid criticism, but if you keep going you also won't miss glorious encounters with God that He has prepared for you and others!

5

SHARING THE MIND OF GOD: THE NEUROLOGY OF REVELATION

People ask me all the time how I hear from God and often look at me in disbelief when I tell them that they too can hear from God in the same way. The Holy Spirit is literally the go-between, overlapping our thoughts with God. Because we share His Spirit, we *can* know the innermost secret thoughts of God.

Chapter two of 1 Corinthians offers an amazing connector passage that reveals our relationship to God. Paul's message to Corinth here is proof that what Jesus prayed for in John 17:24 (that He wants us to be where He is and witness His glory) is possible. For generations in the Old Testament, God rebuked His people for their rebellion, asking them, "Who knows my mind that he may instruct me?" Before Christ, this was often God's response when man reasoned in his own intellect about who He was and the mysterious nature of His ways.

Then in the New Testament, in that game-changing passage (see 1 Cor. 2:10-16), Paul describes what God's intention for His creations was all along: He wants to share His mind with us. He wants us to know the deep things He is thinking and to feel the depths of His heart. Paul even says the Holy Spirit searches the "deepest parts of God" and relates them to us:

> … these are the things God has revealed to us by His Spirit. The Spirit searches all things, even the deep things of God. For who knows a person's thoughts except their own spirit within them? In the same way, no one knows the thoughts of God except the Spirit of God. What we have received is not the spirit of the world but the Spirit who is from God, so that we may understand what God has freely given us. This is what we speak, not in words taught us by human wisdom but in words taught by the Spirit, explaining spiritual realities with Spirit-taught words. The person without the Spirit does not accept the things that come from the Spirit of God but considers them foolishness to him, and cannot understand them because they are discerned only through the Spirit. The person with the Spirit makes judgments about all things, but such a person is not subject to merely human judgments, for, "Who has known the mind of the Lord so as to instruct him?" But we have the mind of Christ (1 Cor. 2: 10-16).

What does it mean to have the mind of Christ or to have the Holy Spirit searching even the deep things of God to reveal them to us?

Before Paul said this to the church at Corinth, this truth had never before been spoken or written. God spent hundreds of years hoping that the people of Israel would know His mind, but in the New Testament He says to believers: *Through Christ, you can know what I'm thinking…you can share my very intention and heart.* He even says that a man who doesn't have a spiritual nature won't understand the importance of this or accept it as truth. To reject this truth is to reject a relationship with God. By imparting His thoughts to us, in the deepest way, God freely and eagerly gives us access to truly understand Him.

SHARING HEADSPACE WITH GOD

I have taught thousands of people through prophetic classes, seminars, conferences, and online courses. One of the first things we do during a hands-on training time is identify how the students there hear from God. Almost everyone's primary way is impressions: You have thoughts or feelings about something that get dropped into your mind or "spirit." Most of the time, it feels like new thoughts you weren't thinking that are suddenly part of your thought process—downloaded thoughts, so to speak. We have the voice of our inner conscience that many times God's voice also shares.

When people ask me how I hear from God, I always think they want to hear these epic stories of biblical proportions. Praise God, I have had some pretty remarkable encounters. But for the most part, I describe hearing from God as sharing the same headspace with Him. I share His mind and thoughts. I've been learning how to discern when those thoughts are His or mine. His thoughts are usually so beautiful and they help me focus on love and my relationship in an organic way because He lives in me. Even as someone who has grown up in the church, my normal human tendency would be to disconnect or disassociate much of the time. But because I choose relationship with Him and others, His thoughts and truth—and even His ability to make the Bible come alive through me—help me to plug in and stay connected and present. Sometimes God sounds like the voice in your head because He lives in you. You can learn how to distinguish when it's you or Him. It might be as simple as identifying selfish versus unselfish desires. Sometimes, it's way more complicated than that.

Have you ever made up your mind about a major life decision and then, through a relational interaction, ended up changing your mind? Having His Spirit inside of us mentors our character and influences our desires, causing us to make very different choices than if we were left to our own thoughts and process, without His inspiration.

We make complicated choices all of the time around our relationships, conflicts, preferences, anxieties, and past experiences.

If we don't know how to grow in our connection to God's heart and mind, this lack of knowledge or practice can cause interruptions and bad choices, or at least lesser choices than the ones we make when we hear God's voice.

Learning how to distinguish your desires and thoughts from His desires and thoughts takes a discerning heart and some self-awareness and emotional intelligence. These are essential skills, because the more you learn to connect to God's thoughts and the revelations of His heart, the more you learn to see past your own opinions and observations in life.

Most of my words of knowledge come as thoughts. Sometimes it's word association, like seeing a friend whom I love when I'm looking at someone else. I can "borrow" from my love and connection to my friend before I talk to this new person. They might share the same name, which happens all of the time. For example, I might see my friend Jeremy and then discover the name of the person I'm ministering to is also called Jeremy. For a few minutes, while I pray or interact with this person, I then get the opportunity to love him like I love my friend.

To really understand the mind of Christ, though, we need to look a little at how the natural mind works.

THE NATURAL-SPIRITUAL CONNECTION THROUGH NEUROLOGY

As I continue to grow in words of knowledge, I find myself wanting to understand more about the connection between the natural and the spiritual. Over the last few years, I've been loosely studying neurology (biology of the brain) and neurobiology (biology of the nervous system) to gain a greater understanding of how this beautiful gift works.

What I'm learning is that the science of the natural mind has parallels with science of the spiritual mind. I can see a similar process to what we experience in our spiritual development. Besides the universe itself, I think our brain's neural network is the most complicated thing God made. Even in creating artificial intelligence, we can only mimic the complicated process. We can't achieve even a fraction of the sophisticated brain patterns and neural interfaces that God freely gave us.

Our mind's ability to process information also acts as a prototype that helps us understand how our spirit processes information, as well. Because we have the mind of Christ, our minds seem to intersect with His. We get downloads, impressions or thoughts that intersect with God's huge, heavenly, loving thoughts, in much the same way our smart devices receive updates to processors.

As soon as I began to go after words of knowledge, I began to receive revelation in a different way to when it was just creative pictures or dreams that had to be interpreted for encouragement. At times, I feel like I'm getting a direct link to the mind of Christ, and I can feel, hear or imagine His thoughts about the world around me. It's like an overlap between His thoughts and mine. Suddenly, I have wisdom that I didn't have before without a spiritual transfusion.

The natural-spiritual parallels become quite clear when we look at what happens in our brains physiologically. Just as we have a neural network that all of our neurons, or brain energy, flows through to create connected thought between our living organs and systems, we also have a spiritual internal network that God's Spirit flows through. Based on different life experiences and ongoing education, neural pathways form as neurons fire in our brains. Neurons create pathways that grow the network of our intelligence and thoughts, connecting our conscious thoughts in more effective ways.

Sometimes, if we have deeper connection on a topic we care about or a connection with someone we care deeply about, our neurons mimic each other and form similar, or nearly the same, types of neural pathways in our brains. These neural pathways also create a similar neural network so that as we interact, we create a similar mental structure, in which neurons fire and interact.

NEURONS THAT FIRE TOGETHER WIRE TOGETHER

In my research, I ran across a phrase first coined in 1949 by Donald Hebb, a Canadian neuropsychologist: "Neurons that fire together wire together." Hebb's axiom reminds us that every experience, thought, feeling and human sensation triggers thousands of neurons, which forms a neural network. Neurons working together strengthen neural connections.

We form covenants or spiritual connections the same way. Experience-triggered neural firing is how *all* neural pathways become patterns of response and how *all* structures of the brain mature.

One of my favorite studies comes from Daniel Siegel, a neurologist at UCLA who is pioneering new thought in the neurobiological community, by discussing interpersonal neurobiology. He says that the brain is the only organ in the body developed by social interaction. In his study, Siegel explores how interacting with others affects us neurobiologically as we grow and age.

"On the individual level, the neurons in the limbic regions—the seat of our emotional learning that's foundational to our subjective sense of personal and social self—are not fully connected at birth," Siegel writes in his book *The Neurobiology of "We": How Relationships, the Mind and the Brain Interact to Shape Who We Are.*[1] "They are genetically primed to form synaptic connections through the relational experiences we have with those closest to us."

These early connections happen through our parents, or what neurobiologists call "caregivers". Siegel says that caregivers activate the growth of these regions in the brain through emotional availability and reciprocal interactions. This includes the hormones of bonding and pleasure released in intimate relationships. This is how all patterns of attachment are laid down in the brain; it's also how they can change. Siegel explains, "Patterns of energy and information laid down in these early moments of meeting develop the actual structure of these limbic regions [where we do our emotional learning]."[2]

[1] *The Pocket Guide to Interpersonal Neurobilogy* || Chapter 19
[2] *Trauma called Healing Trauma* || Daniel Siegel

This means that the very foundations of perception, particularly in regards to relationships, rely on the quality of these early interactions with our parents.

Think about that in light of God's caregiving nature toward us and how He develops us, not only outside and spiritually but also inside and mentally. Now that we know the brain is a socially developed organ, we can understand that, as a caregiver to our spiritual mind, God is allowing our process of spiritual thought to form along the same lines as His own way of thinking.

As we pray and read the Bible and connect to what He is saying, God's mind and our mind begin to wire together! It's not just an invisible thing; our neurological network actually expands. Both our brain and our spirit mature together.

And with other believers? We share biblical foundational ideas and God's heart. Suddenly, we have an inner spiritual network that comes alive with spiritual neurons traveling down our spiritual network to create a deep life in God's Spirit.

So, you can see that if we parallel the neurobiology of our minds with that of our spiritual minds, the interaction with God as our primary caregiver creates a whole framework for how our spiritual mind responds. It will only develop through interaction with Him, through His Word and His Spirit.

This creates a synergy of relationship, where our experience as a Christian, with God as our caregiver and nurturer through His Spirit, forms a structure of His character and personhood inside of us. In this kind of relationship, our thoughts wire together with His thoughts.

We were created as relational and social beings, to be connected on a mental, physical, and spiritual level. This small picture of neurobiology I've laid out only goes to show you how deeply this relational connection matters spiritually.

Let me show you how this plays out in real life. A few years ago, I was at dinner with some friends who were visiting from Southeast

Asia. They had brought a friend who was a hedge fund director. This man was brilliant in his Ivy League training and his very developed financial experience. We began to talk, and I felt like God showed me, *He hasn't had any Christian who has ever understood him or the way he thinks, but I gave him this mind for finances. I am going to give you wisdom and revelation so that he can feel a connection to My mind and heart.*

We began a conversation about financial markets and for the next hour, I talked as if I was a fellow expert. I knew trends in finances, commodity markets, and banking information that only people in private equity or hedge funds would have been privy to. I could tell he was enjoying himself as we went back and forth, developing a Kingdom perspective of the financial world. Honestly, our conversation felt like a therapy session and wisdom impartation for him and also expanded me in some subjects I would have never even thought about without his brilliance.

When he left the table, my friend looked at me and asked, "Okay, what's going on? We've known you forever, and you know *nothing* about what you're talking about. And I know you haven't had time to study. Is God just possessing you? You sound like you should be consulting with all of Wall Street right now."

I began to laugh when I thought back to our conversation. I had sounded so brilliant and so connected to the financial world, but now it was gone. I could feel traces of God's mind and those huge thoughts in my mind, but it was like He overlapped my mind so that I could understand and speak about something that was just far bigger than I could think of or imagine. I didn't have the slightest bit of education or experience to be talking about and comprehending finances on that level.

When their friend came back to the table, he was beaming. "I just feel like I have had the conversation of a lifetime!" he said.

I was able to share with him what had happened and how God wanted to relate to him and let him know that his mind and way of thinking are Kingdom gifts to the world. He was teary-eyed and just felt so understood and loved by God. To this day, though, he's convinced that I'm a financial genius.

OUR MIND AND GOD'S: WIRING AND FIRING TOGETHER

As I stressed above, our mind is firing with God's and is wiring with His mind. The more we develop our connection to Him through the revelation gifts, our social spiritual activity, and through reading the Bible, the more our spiritual and mental neural network get expanded and make room for more neurons and the spiritual light to travel. Don't let the word "light" scare you. I'm not talking about trying to reach a place of enlightenment like so many religions do. We obtain knowledge by faith in Jesus as a free gift that's already developing in us.

Understanding that we're changed through God's mental process firing with ours is a huge leap forward in our faith. Jesus constantly surprised the Pharisees by proposing different options than those they brought to Him (e.g. "Whoever doesn't have sin, go ahead and cast the first stone" (John 8:7) "Give back to Caesar what is Caesar's" (Mark 12:17)). There are dozens of these stories. Jesus would be sharing the mind of God and, like Solomon, He would come up with outrageous wisdom. The Word was alive in Him. He didn't just have knowledge but also God's intention over each Scripture, so that when He used Scripture, it was a manifestation of His nature, not just words.

Several years ago, during a church service in Singapore where I was ministering, I called out a woman's name and through a word of knowledge knew her birthday.

"You have a dog that you lost," I said to her. She shook her head no, but I continued. "I see this dog named Rick, he was always biting you and running off and scratching and biting your kids. But he has run away for good and can no longer hurt you and the kids. Let him go; you will never find him again. God has something better for you than a dog."

As I shared with her, she cried the whole time. Later, she came up to me and the pastor and told us, "I don't have a dog named Rick. I have a husband named Rick who has been womanizing and has basically abandoned us. I have been praying for restoration, but your word helped me realize that after twenty years, he's not going to stop having affairs and that I need to protect myself and my family. God is good. I feel delivered."

Now I would have never called a person a dog, nor would I have given a word to discourage marriage. I'm too positive for that. But obviously, God knew how to get through to this precious lady and help her because she couldn't come to a decision in her very abusive relationship. He did it in such a creative way that she wasn't exposed, and I didn't even know what was happening.

Words of knowledge are not dependent on your disposition, your thoughts, your understanding, or even your emotional intelligence or biblical interpretation of theology. Just as Peter said he couldn't eat unclean foods that God told him to eat because it was against the rules of his faith—instead of the Lord of His faith—sometimes we follow our relationship with God and it actually proves the nature of the Bible that we have previously misunderstood.

We have a spiritual mind that's intimately developed and connected through our relationship with others. As Paul says, we literally have the mind of Christ and, as His mind develops in us, we start to grow in our capacity to have wisdom, revelations, and profound ideas that can shape the world around us.

There are times when I have sat down with people and had a true divine moment, where I felt as though I wasn't limited to my own brain and ideas. But I can *feel* God's mind overlapping with mine, as if I have a higher consciousness that allows me to relate to someone in a place of love, empathy, compassion, wisdom, and insight. I'm not just the human version of me. I'm enlightened by the mind of the Father in heaven who has original thoughts and ideas about everyone and everything He has created.

God sent His Son to restore us to His original plan, and Jesus has very real thoughts about this for each one of us, as well as each geographical region, each industry, and each people group. These are deeply thought-out plans, with full resources from heaven. As a Christian, the closer we get to God in really knowing Him, the more opportunity we have to catch up with these thoughts and to have them shared with us—to the point that they affect our core.

WORDS OF KNOWLEDGE PAINT A PICTURE OF GOD

I love the idiom "A picture is worth a thousand words." In some ways, a good prophetic message is worth a thousand sermons. It can motivate us and stimulate our relational connection with God in a way that few other relational tools from heaven can. One word picture can be so defining for someone. One word picture or pun, one action word or phrase that defines a moment in someone's life, can become identity building.

A few years ago, I was with friends having dinner, and one of my friend's business associates showed up with his brother. We all shared a big table together. As I talked with the business associate, he began to pour his heart out about how hard and bad his marriage was.

"I would never leave her but she is so bitter," he said through tears.

Two things happened. I saw a woman I used to work with who I will call Janet. I thought maybe this might mean something to him. Then I also saw two people making out in a classic Ford car late at night (not in detail, more like a vague memory of a movie I'd seen). But I also thought I would ask him about that.

"I think God wants to give you some hope about your marriage," I told Him. "He designed marriage to be a huge source of life for us. Who is Janet?"

His eyes got wide, and he had to review the stories he had told us that night to see if he had said her name. He hadn't.

"That is my wife," he said.

"God knows your situation," I told him. "She is the right one for you, and He wants to give you guys another chance at romance."

Then I told him about the car and seeing a young couple make out in the old Ford. He started laughing and got a twinkle in his eye.

"We had our first date in my dad's old Ford, and it was love at the first date. I kept kissing her so much, and she kept saying, 'If you want to kiss me anymore, you are going to have to marry me.' I was so in love with her, and I did marry her!"

"God is reminding you of the love you once had because you can have it again," I told him. He began to cry again, but this time there was hope.

"I guess I've got to pursue her like I did in that old Ford," he laughed.

I saw him several months later, and he gave me a big ol' bear hug and related how he and his wife had both given up on the marriage but that something in our conversation that night had rekindled the pursuit. They were also going to church as a family for the first time in twenty years.

I hadn't really said much to him that night, but what was said played at the chords of identity and connection in his heart. That is what revelation does: It reveals what is necessary. Sometimes it reveals something that's in the way (like a womanizing husband named Rick) and other times it shines light on what's wonderful but forgotten (like love on a first date). Revelation gives us a perfect picture of God's heart and mind.

GOD'S MIND IS PERFECT IN ITS PSYCHOLOGY AND NEUROLOGY

One of the things I love about the idea of sharing headspace with God is that it renews our mind. Romans 12:1-2 talks about the renewing of our mind when we connect to God. *The Message* version clearly lays out how God develops well-formed maturity in us:

> *So here's what I want you to do, God helping you: Take your everyday, ordinary life—your sleeping, eating, going-to-work, and walking around life—and place it before God as an offering. Embracing what God does for you is the best thing you can do for him. Don't become so well adjusted to your culture that you fit into it without even thinking. Instead, fix your attention on God. You'll be changed from the inside out. Readily recognize what he wants from you, and quickly respond to it. Unlike the culture around you, always dragging you down to its level of immaturity, God brings the best out of you, develops well-formed maturity in you (Rom. 12:1-2).*

Have you ever had a mentor or a really good teacher? Your knowledge isn't the only thing that grows as a result of this person's influence. Your thinking changes. You can make better choices with clearer and more obvious outcome possibilities. When the Holy Spirit is living in you, He helps you disciple your thoughts. I feel like people who are really sharing those deep thoughts with God are marked by the fruit of the connection Paul lays out in Galatians 5:

> *But what happens when we live God's way? He brings gifts into our lives, much the same way that fruit appears in an orchard— things like affection for others, exuberance about life, serenity. We develop a willingness to stick with things, a sense of compassion in the heart, and a conviction that a basic holiness permeates things and people. We find ourselves involved in*

loyal commitments, not needing to force our way in life, able to marshal and direct our energies wisely.

Legalism is helpless in bringing this about; it only gets in the way. Among those who belong to Christ, everything connected with getting our own way and mindlessly responding to what every one else calls necessities is killed off for good—crucified (Gal. 5:22-24, The Message).

GOD OPENS THE DEPTHS AND TELLS THEIR SECRETS

When the goal of revelation is to connect God's mind and heart to the world around us, it creates a holy peer pressure to honor people and groups (e.g. businesses, governments, and countries) that we would normally judge either in our own human thoughts or by our own religious convictions. I think of how Daniel was given spiritual knowledge, but he didn't become a separatist from Babylonian society. Instead, he became one of the most powerful men in the nation. He followed his relationship with God in a way that was, for sure controversial to other Jews, but in the end, it saved him and his friends. Let's look at Daniel 2:19-23:

That night the answer to the mystery was given to Daniel in a vision. Daniel blessed the God of heaven, saying,

Blessed be the name of God,
forever and ever.
He knows all, does all:
He changes the seasons and guides history,
He raises up kings and also brings them down,
He provides both intelligence and discernment,
He opens up the depths, tells secrets,
sees in the dark—light spills out of him!

God of all my ancestors, all thanks! All praise!
You made me wise and strong.
And now you've shown us what we asked for.
You've solved the king's mystery.

In essence, Daniel gets a prophetic message from the mind of God to solve the king's mystery. Can you imagine if we pursued an intimacy with God that produced the solutions to the most critical problems or mysteries in society today?

On top of that, Daniel asked the king not to kill the Babylonian astrologers. Modern Christianity often makes the error of wanting to shut everyone else down. But when love comes through truth, conversion happens. Daniel knew that God showing up through him provided all kinds of Babylonians with an invitation to connect to this amazing God. He had compassion for them.

Solomon perhaps gives us the greatest picture of someone who flowed with the wisdom of the mind of God through revelation and understanding. The greatest thinkers of the world took pilgrimages just to sit in Solomon's court to see how he deliberated and made decisions. He constantly baffled his citizens and visitors with the way he presided over his people. Think about the two women in 1 Kings 3:16 who come to him fighting over a baby, both claiming to be its mother. Solomon's mind is working on a higher frequency when he proposes this resolution: "Let's cut the baby in half and you can each take a piece!" In his wisdom, he knew the real mother couldn't bear it and would refuse to let that happen.

In 1 Kings 10:9 (*The Message*), the Queen of Sheba says to Solomon, "*And blessed be God, your God, who took such a liking to you and made you king. Clearly, God's love for Israel is behind this, making you king to keep a just order and nurture a God-pleasing people.*"

The queen recognized that the God of Israel was real, loved His people, and poured knowledge and wisdom into Solomon as a sign of His nurturing love for His people. In other words, because Solomon operated in the Spirit of revelation and had these words of knowledge and wisdom, he brought the most powerful queen in the world to conversion.

This is what sharing God's mind does. It produces revelation, knowledge and wisdom that baffles the world—not by its complexity but by its demonstration that God is real and loves the world.

6

PURSUING A LIFESTYLE OF RISK

One of the steps to getting more and more from God is to be faithful and to take a risk—even when it feels like what you have is insignificant or silly.

A few months ago, I was in Dallas (my new favorite city) on my way to film a TV show, in the backseat in a car with an extremely chatty Uber driver. I had only gotten five hours of sleep the night before and was pre-coffee, so I wasn't really that interested in talking. Fortunately, he was kind enough to swing by and let me get a cup of coffee, which seemed to be what I needed to focus a little and listen during the forty-five minute drive.

As we drove, he shared about some of his life and the financial crises that had pushed him into taking a second job with Uber. He was actually a lawyer in his native country and had tried to start an immigration law business in Dallas, but there had been so many obstacles.

As we talked, I got a heart for Him and knowing I may never see him again, began to ask God for anything for him. I had a thought in my head that formed an unfamiliar word: "Edma". I didn't know what that could mean, but I heard it clearly.

We were about fifteen minutes out from the studio, and I just asked him, "Does E-D-M-A mean anything to you?" He began to look around the car and then, smiling, asked, "How do you know my wife's name?"

Then I had a flood of God's thoughts and began to minister to him about his wife and their marriage and family. He was so overwhelmed he had to pull over. I was so touched by God's heart for him. It was like I had taken a backseat to God, as He took over the steering wheel and just led the journey. At the end of our very personal time, I asked him, "Do you have a relationship with Jesus?" He said he was religious but didn't have a relationship with Him. I led him in a wonderful state with Jesus Christ, and we both were so joyful.

GROWING REQUIRES PRACTICE AND RISK

Dear friends, do you think you'll get anywhere in this if you learn all the right words but never do anything? Does merely talking about faith indicate that a person really has it? For instance, you come upon an old friend dressed in rags and half-starved and say, "Good morning, friend! Be clothed in Christ! Be filled with the Holy Spirit!" and walk off without providing so much as a coat or a cup of soup—where does that get you? Isn't it obvious that God-talk without God-acts is outrageous nonsense?

I can already hear one of you agreeing by saying, "Sounds good. You take care of the faith department, I'll handle the works department."

Not so fast. You can no more show me your works apart from your faith than I can show you my faith apart from my works. Faith and works, works and faith, fit together hand in glove (James 2: 14-17, The Message).

James tells us that to grow in our faith, we must take action. Otherwise, it's a lifeless faith. It makes sense. When we actually act on our faith, we activate it. We demonstrate our beliefs. If you say you love your kids or spouse but do nothing to show it, an take no personal risks for them, saying you love them begins to sound hollow.

Some of your greatest moments of risk with revelation will feel like they aren't going to be worth it. People often ask me how I learned to take risks. The truth is, I've battled deep insecurity in my lifetime and, after pursuing healing, therapy, and identity, I'm now on the winning side of the battle, thank God! So many times, those insecurities crippled me when I even thought about taking a risk and sharing.

Looking back, those insecurities were somewhat irrational, driven partly by our family moving every few years and having to start over with new friends and new schools, and partly by my desire for significance and worth. I was so self-conscious, always reading into their actions and words to determine if they liked me. That lack of self-confidence compelled me to please people as much as possible, spending extra energy to gain the approval I probably already had. I remember sharing my heart or something that was important to me and just feeling like what I'd talked about was dumb and insignificant.

When you apply insecurity to the prophetic, you wind up with a lot of spiritual self-doubt. Because I wanted to make sure the person I was sharing with really accepted my words as spiritual encouragement, I would often exaggerate—which is just counterproductive. I would also give words and then feel totally defeated afterwards, even when the person I was sharing with had a positive response. Insecurity caused me to feel like what I said wasn't valuable or worth saying. If you don't already know it, insecurity is a real thief! I loved when I overcame it through the love of Jesus!

I still remember the beginning of my breakthrough. I was toying with taking a risk, but could feel the fear starting to take over when this thought fired into my head: *Will you feel better by not taking the risk and having a normal life, or by taking the risk and possibly seeing something awesome happen?*

I had witnessed other people accessing God in awesome ways many times, so I knew it was possible. But the risk process seemed so daunting. Still, I knew I had to try to begin to open myself up to taking risks to share what God was giving me, and to see His hand move in unfathomable ways.

The bottom line is that if you want to grow in hearing from God—especially in the black-and-white process of words of knowledge—you'll have to learn to take risks. Many times, my friends and I will do a growth activation. I'll think of someone I know well but my friend doesn't know at all, and he'll do the same and then we'll begin to pray. Then we ask yes or no questions about them: "Is it a man?" "Is it an older person?" "Are they a nurse?" "Are they from New York?" Sometimes, it feels like a guessing game. That is, until it doesn't. We go until we get two to three correct words of knowledge, and then we pray for them with faith. Sometimes, prophetic words come out of it so we can give them later. This is just one of the many, many intentional methods we have used to grow in hearing specifics from God.

What I love about this type of practice is that you learn to discern when it's just your thoughts or guesses from when it's God. Some people have an instinct for this, but for many of us, God is renewing our minds, so there's a process of learning about how to connect to God's thoughts. It took me years of practice before I felt confident. Still, my confidence doesn't mean I'm great at this. It just means I'm confidently learning.

At one point, I was confident in the specific ways God was speaking to me, and then He changed it on me. I realize now I was turning it into a function, not a relational tool. It felt like God made the risk-taking more difficult to challenge me to go after more. I remember being in a meeting in Anaheim and during a prophetic ministry time I heard, "monkey power, one, two, three." And that was all. Can you imagine speaking into a microphone and asking if something like that meant anything to anyone? The room looked at me for just a second and then someone screamed. It was a girl whose username was Monkeypower123 in junior high school. A few of her friends remembered it and were laughing.

Another time, at Bethel Church in Redding, California, I heard the name "Bootsy Bugs." It felt like a cartoon name, and I thought, "*Well, it's either a character in someone's book they're writing or someone has a really unique name.*" I didn't know if it was even real, but because I had taken risks thousands of times in stores, at theaters, at coffee shops and in prayer lines, I was willing to take the risk. I had nothing else to go off of and nothing to lose.

"I don't know if this is a character's name or a dog's name or a person," I told the crowd, "but is there a Bootsy Bugs here?"

Immediately, I heard a loud gasp or scream from a young man. He couldn't believe God knew his nickname. After the revelation of his name was shown to be real, the rest of the word came to me, and it was so meaningful and wonderful.

God wants interdependence from us, not self-reliance. He puts us in a place of risk-taking so that we will connect to—and stay connected to—Him.

I MISSED FIVE IN A ROW

So, what happens when we take a risk and don't see an immediate payoff? In 2016, I went to Dallas and experienced one of my new favorite churches (actually, I visited several amazing churches in Dallas and now think that Dallas probably has one of the best Christian cultures in the world). This particular church was called Upper Room. Up until then, everywhere I'd gone, for the entire year, felt like a homerun and was exciting to the max. Then I got to this church and tried to prophesy using words of knowledge. I tried one thing I was seeing, but no one responded. Then I called out the name of a couple and got nothing. After five attempts, I started laughing. This group who was new to me had just watched me fumble. There was no recovery except for the humility of my own humanity.

"Well, folks, you just watched me try and take risks; it's never easy but it is worth it when it happens," I told the crowd. "Maybe some of you can identify with risk-taking, and I hope you will still go for it. Sometimes it won't pay off but when it does, it's huge dividends!"

I felt very vulnerable trying these five readings without the relational connection that I've grown to love. But I still had a great time. After the meeting, a young woman came up to me.

"I have to tell you something, and I hope I don't offend you," she said. "I've seen videos of you before tonight and thought what you were doing was a mentalist or circus act. I thought you were researching people online and just had a lot of ego. I had judged you as a fake and wanted to come tonight so that I could protect my friends and debrief with them later."

"But tonight, you weren't right at all! And you didn't have to be right. Someone who was faking it wouldn't be wrong that many times. They would make sure they got *something*. You didn't hit anything with your risks. Then afterwards you led us in prayer and still encouraged us. I just felt God's love through you and now believe that what you do is real. It took me seeing you miss for me to realize you have no ego or performance issues in needing to hear from God."

Because I failed so miserably and didn't try and cover it up or make it look better, this young girl believed. It was what it was, and I just had to own it. Quite a few times, this has happened. I've taken a risk in front of friends or in a meeting, but it not working out has been almost as powerful as when I'm able to give someone a revelation.

TAKE RESPONSIBILITY AND MOVE ON

If you're taking risks to share words of knowledge, then you too will likely experience the same thing. Your risks won't pay off every time, for various reasons you may never understand. Each time, however, you'll learn, whatever the outcome. Revelatory gifts and words of knowledge are a social experiment. To spiritually encourage someone, you have to share with another human. If something doesn't make sense or if you've "missed" it, what happens next?

It's pretty simple. You practice humility. You say, "Thanks for letting me try that." Or, "Oops! I'm learning." You don't have to be deeply repentant. Then you try again the next day or the next time. Can you imagine if every time kids tried to play the piano, they had to stop and loudly repent each time they missed a note? We'd have no musicians. They just try it again until they get it right. They adapt, practice, and change, which is true repentance anyway.

It's so important that you don't make too big a deal out of misses. Just take responsibility when it's necessary. After all, it's a relational process in the first place. Don't create social awkwardness or draw more attention to yourself. I believe so strongly in this that I'm giving you two personal examples (good versus bad) of how to take responsibility when you take risks and miss.

Good example: Recently, I went up to a woman at the mall and asked her if she was in between jobs. She said, "No, why?". I knew I had either misread what I was feeling or hearing or that there was nothing to begin with and I needed to just move on. I made a quick choice to follow it up.

"Well, I'm a Christian and felt God's heart for you. Can I try again? Are you doing what you feel you were made for?"

She gave me a chance: "Definitely not! I work as an assistant to a tax preparation company. This is *not* my dream job."

I told her, "I just sensed that God wants to help you do what you're made for, so can I pray with you?"

She was super happy and not weirded out at all. She felt my connection and was glad to have me pray for her and her future.

Bad example: A gas company man came to the house, and I asked him if his mother had a rare type of cancer.

"No, why?" I could tell he thought it was a terribly weird question. I didn't know what to say.

"Um, I'm a Christian and thought maybe your mom was sick and that I should pray for her or you. I am so sorry! I was just trying to hear from God. Wow, sorry, um, is anyone sick?"

"No!" he said, visibly frustrated. He got out of there faster than you can imagine.

I babbled in a way that made him feel disconnected from me and, therefore, away from the God in me. In hindsight, I could have just asked, "Are you concerned for any of your family's health?"

The prophetic gifts are connecting gifts. Words of knowledge may not work out each time, but you should be able to fall back on your social skills that you're madly working on to be love to the world. When it comes to the revelation gifts, people who don't work on their emotional intelligence, self-awareness, heart and relational health are often very frustrating to walk with, as they substitute information for their lack of identity and relational connection.

RISKING WITH YOUR LIFE AND TIME

Think about it. God wants to give you words of knowledge that actually change the course of not only others' lives and purposes, but also your own. Paul was on his second missionary journey, at a standstill (the Spirit had already redirected them twice) in Troas, when he had a clear vision of a man in Macedonia begging for him to come. God powerfully gave Paul a word of knowledge that the Macedonian people were ready to receive the gospel and, as a result, Paul changed his travel plans, entering into one of his most fruitful times of ministry.

I remember God giving my wife and I a word of knowledge during a financially uncertain season. I was releasing a new book, and we had to decide how many books to order. We were dealing with a very limited budget, but knew we needed to put considerable resources into this project. Our publisher also was buying books, but we resource our own events and website and needed to know how many books to buy. When Cherie and I received the same number, we put in the order.

That word of knowledge gave us the faith we needed to risk the time and money we had invested in this project. We felt like we knew not only what God wanted, but also what our market would need. As small business owners, that word of knowledge was essential. When the book was released it was the perfect number, and we sold through the books in record time. But if we had bought more, we would have had a storage problem. If we had bought less, we would have had to make an expensive emergency order.

Another time, while in Africa, our car was detained by some fake police, and the Lord showed me they were trying to take illegal bribes and to not be afraid of their guns. I then got a word for a man about his mother and took the risk to share with him. He was so shocked that he let me pray with him and then sent us on without further threats.

A RELATIONAL, NOT METHODOLICAL, PROCESS

Sometimes, we discount how much our relational process with others is also a creative process. You can't teach someone how to fall in love with the exact person they end up with, but you can give them relational tools and set helpful boundaries for keeping that love safe and healthy.

If you take a methodological approach to hearing from God, it just won't work. I referred to this earlier in Chapter 2, but even Jesus said, in Matthew 13:

> *That's why I tell stories: to create readiness, to nudge the people toward receptive insight. In their present state, they can stare till doomsday and not see it, listen till they're blue in the face and not get it* (Matt. 13:13, The Message).

Sometimes when we want to tell someone something from our heart, we don't use direct words. Instead, we use ideas and word pictures to share how we're feeling. Anyone who's learning how to translate a language knows that effective translation is not just about translating the words. You need to be more comprehensive, able to translate a concept or thought and present it, so that nothing gets lost in translation.

God speaks to us in many ways, and some people get frustrated that He's not always more direct. In every relationship, there's a learning curve that takes time to overcome, that actually points toward the intimacy there. You can only say, "I know you!" to someone you're invested in, someone with whom you've shared your beliefs, heart, sentiment, and even humor. When done wrong, religion tries to ritualize or even sidestep the relational process, which is actually the very thing that makes true faith beautiful.

VAGUE VERSUS SPECIFIC

Some of my words of knowledge lean on being very specific, but it wasn't always that way. Nor did I (or do I) always know when words I received were going to be that specific. I would say something like, "I see a horse running." And then the person would later give me feedback that they owned a horse ranch and that I had used the exact language of their hobby or passion.

I gradually learned to look for these indicators and dig deeper into them, or at least acknowledge them as different to when I only received a concept related word picture. I believe that the more we can identify with these direct connections, the more we can start to let our faith and spirit operate deliberately towards repeating these kinds of events.

While we all want an Acts 10 Cornelius experience (where an angel visits and tells him exactly who to talk to and what to do), there is still the relational process of walking something out.

The reality is that a relationship takes time and when we start to hear from God, it feels vague at first. We might have Cornelius encounters in our life from time to time, but until we mature into the place of connected relationship to ourselves, to God, and to the world around us, the revelation process can feel awkward. We need to embrace this awkward period, though, just like a teen discovering the opposite sex! This is an exciting, albeit awkward, time in life that we shouldn't skip or bypass! Even the disciples didn't understand Jesus most of the time. They constantly asked Him what He meant. In fact, it took them three years of walking and living life with Him to start to understand Him. Toward the end of His ministry on Earth, they told Him, "Finally, you're giving it to us straight, in plain talk—no more figures of speech. Now we know that you know everything—it all comes together in you …" (John 16:29, *The Message*).

Who really changed? Jesus or the disciples? The disciples just hadn't caught up to the fact that after all of the time they had invested with Jesus, they finally "got" Him. They now knew how to listen, even to His abstract language and concepts, because overtime their hearts had become attuned to His heart by being with and connecting to Jesus. When we continue to stay in a relationship with God, the vague begins to feel more specific.

THE PROPHETIC CREATES A NEED FOR RELATIONSHIP

In this age of instant gratification, our human nature is to want what we want *now*. We can get so many things on demand. Everything can be delivered or expedited to the point that in the Western world, we constantly bypass relationship for convenience. No wonder we're the most starved for love we have ever been as a society.

When you begin to engage the prophetic and see fruit from those risks, you start to see how desperate people are to connect with God. Often, you get good people but with misplaced desires. As we talked about in Chapter 4, they tend to just look for you to use words of knowledge to solve their problems. Each week, I receive hundreds of emails from people asking to have their problems fixed. They want God to wave a magic wand over their life, which many times took lots of poor choices to even get there in the first place. It's like saying to your personal trainer, "Why am I not skinny yet? I worked out yesterday!" Anyone who has worked hard at something knows that one workout might be a step toward good shape but only if it's laid on a foundation of a lifestyle change.

The prophetic does bring breakthrough moments in life. It can bring tipping points. It can help simplify, or even bring solutions, to problems. But ultimately, hearing from God is about knowing and relating to Him and having the faith to take risks—not just so that things go better for you or the people with whom you're sharing.

Often prophecy exposes what God wants to do in our lives. It actually makes us aware of the gap between our desires and His. The prophetic radically matures us relationally. So, words of knowledge and knowing the secrets of God are primarily for relationship, and then secondarily, they do a work through us to the world around us.

Before words of knowledge focus on when the economy will get better or worse, they reveal that God is with you and knows you in a real way. This idea is stunning to unbelievers and fulfills what Paul wrote in his first letter to the church of Corinth: "But if all prophesy, and an unbeliever or outsider enters, he is convicted by all, he is called to account by all, the secrets of his heart are disclosed, and so, falling on his face, he will worship God and declare that God is really among you" (1 Cor. 14:24, ESV).

I love this passage. It reminds me that an unbeliever or a spiritual outsider can hear from God and be transformed through words of knowledge. As they hear the secret in their heart expressed, they respond to the truth that God knows their innermost thoughts. He knows what is precious and important. When it comes to really sharing and taking risks with people, this is a game changer. What if the small phrase you receive is the next entrepreneurial Silicon Valley idea that God has planted in someone's heart? What if the word is about their ill stepchild who's battling for her life and God shows you the slightest medical detail? As 1 Corinthians tells us, when we take the risk to enter into the relational process, everyone around us has the opportunity to witness the truth revealed in someone's life—revelation that has an unbeliever "falling on his face" in worship to the God who interacts with His creation.

From the beginning to the end, God can see everything. He is Alpha and Omega, and because His heart is for us as His heirs, He is concerned with it all. I think of Peter and how Jesus tells him that in one night he will deny Him three times. Peter doesn't realize that this is a prophecy and denies it, saying, "I would *never!*"

Outside of a relationship, this is such an awkward prophetic word. It's hard to imagine what Peter must have felt when the person he had started to realize was God—the person he had walked with for three years—told him he's not going to make it. But when we look at it from a relationship perspective, we see how Jesus' words to Peter reveal a God who loves unconditionally. Jesus was so kind and loved Peter so much that He wanted him to know, "Peter, I love you no matter what, even if in your immaturity, you make a mistake." Peter couldn't really hear what Jesus was saying to him that day. It wasn't until the resurrected Jesus found him fishing naked that He began to understand. Desperately ashamed of his denial, Peter had walked away from everything and had essentially gone back to his old life as a fisherman.

"Peter, do you love Me?" Jesus asked him. "Then feed My sheep."

Instead of rebuking His disciple or reminding him of his denial and asking him to take direct responsibility for it, Jesus gave Peter a mission and, in doing so, communicated His great love for him. Peter felt completely disqualified for anything related to ministry. Jesus knew that. But out of a relationship, we see Peter restored and, ultimately, used by God in powerful ways. We serve a one-of-a-kind God who cares so deeply about our relationship with Him that He looks for ways to connect with us and share His heart.

RISKING FOR GOD HAS LIFE-CHANGING POTENTIAL

One of my favorite stories in Scripture is from Mark, who tells us about the woman with the issue of blood. She was so desperate to be healed she made a public spectacle of herself. Read her story and look for the risks she took:

> And a woman was there who had been subject to bleeding for twelve years. She had suffered a great deal under the care of many doctors and had spent all she had, yet instead of getting better she grew worse. When she heard about Jesus, she came up behind him in the crowd and touched his cloak, because she thought, "If I just touch his clothes, I will be healed." Immediately, her bleeding stopped and she felt in her body that she was freed from her suffering.
>
> At once Jesus realized that power had gone out from him. He turned around in the crowd and asked, "Who touched my clothes?"
>
> "You see the people crowding against you," his disciples answered, 'and yet you can ask, 'Who touched me?'"
>
> But Jesus kept looking around to see who had done it. Then the woman, knowing what had happened to her, came and fell at his feet and, trembling with fear, told him the whole truth. He said to her, "Daughter, your faith has healed you. Go in peace and be freed from your suffering" (Mark 5:25-34).

I love her faith. Let's look at her real story. She had spent all of her money and had no other hope. In Jewish society, the type of disorder she suffered from would label her as "unclean." Touching a holy man like Jesus would have been considered a criminal act punishable by death. But she was so desperate, so believing, that she figured it was worth the risk.

Jesus turns around to the crowd, who had just been pushing into Him and asks, "Who touched Me?" He had a word of knowledge that one of the people who had touched Him had been healed in this moment. The disciples respond incredulously, saying that *everyone* has touched Him. But Jesus knew something special had happened and continued to survey the crowd. The woman felt her body being freed from her suffering and in that moment courageously said, "It was me."

Now this was a small region, and she had been a wealthy woman that many people would have known. They also might have known about the specific health battle she had or at least that she had spent her money but was losing everything as her health continued to deteriorate. She would have been a very known person with a very personal issue. When Jesus spoke out of great faith that something was different in this crowd, He put her on display yet didn't condemn her for touching Him. Instead, He said to her, "Your faith has healed you!"

How amazing is that? The whole crowd probably had restored respect for her. When we recognize God in the moment and take a risk, He can use us to change someone's whole world and trajectory.

I still remember being at my friend's son's soccer game when God used me to transform the life of a hurting, at-risk tween. It seemed like every kid on the field had a parent cheering for him, but no one was there for this kid. He wasn't doing so well in the game and a few times he made some mistakes. You could tell his teammates were getting visibly frustrated with him.

During the break, I went over to my friend's son and asked him about the kid.

"We don't really talk much," he told me. "He seems kind of weird."

I walked over to the young boy and in front of all the team asked him, "What's your ranking in Call of Duty?" It's a pretty mature video game, but I had a word of knowledge about him. He smiled at me and came alive, wondering how I knew of his achievement. He shared his rank, which was one of the top scores in the nation. The other kids were shocked and gathered around him to figure out how he was that awesome.

In one moment, this guy went from being the kid no one saw anything special in to being the center of attention. That one moment redefined his time on his soccer team. Beyond that, my friend told me this kid ended up being one of his son's best friends that year. They brought him to church, and he was saved. Later, his friend told him about how it was a word of knowledge that led me to ask him that question. The kid was amazed.

Time and again, I've seen how God uses this gift to change our world and bring us back to His heart. It's probably my favorite part of practicing words of knowledge and taking risks. I often think about a woman I will call Emery. She was desperate to speak to me after a meeting. Her husband had just left her, and they were in financial ruin. She had nothing left. Even her dog was dying.

She came to me, not just wanting a word of encouragement. She looked at me as though I could fix everything. Like the woman with the blood issue, Emery was looking for a moment that would help her life go back to normal. Her finances would no longer be cursed. Her alcoholic husband would be set free. Her marriage would be restored.

As she poured out her heart, I hugged her. I knew she wanted me to be Jesus and find a way to just make the pain go away. The problem is, I'm not Jesus, and Jesus isn't in the habit of making choices for us. We actually have to come into His grace and start the process of a relationship where we surrender our life to His goodness and make thousands of choices to protect our heart, our life, our relationships, our finances, and our well-being. This is by no means a quick process. Even if God delivers some from everything (He is the beautiful deliverer), others find themselves wandering in a wilderness for a while to gain the connection to God that brings about a personal Promised Land.

I prayed with Emery and gave her a prophetic word: "God is going to give you a buyer for your house and help you to have a place to go to call home. It will be much smaller than what you're used to, but your creativity will come alive there. I saw 'Sycamore.'"

I could tell she was angry.

"I don't *want* my house to sell! I'm near foreclosure, but I have other prophetic words that God is going to save my house. It is on Sycamore Street! I love my home!"

She left me with all the frustration she had toward God manifesting in anger toward me. *I wish I got paid for this,* I thought. *At least DMV workers get paid directly to be yelled at for what they do* (just kidding).

Two years later, Emery came up to me in a meeting. I quickly remembered her. It's not easy to forget someone who's made such a scene. Her countenance was a little different, but you can never really tell what someone is about to say. So, I was on guard.

"Can I have a minute of your time?" she asked me. I braced myself to be an unpaid DMV worker again but welcomed her over, fending off conference security.

"So, right after I talked with you, I sold my house. I was days away from foreclosure. I ended up renting a guest house and at first was so broken and mad at God and you and everyone. The woman who used to live there was an artist and had left some supplies, and I began to paint again like when I was young. I was an art major in college before I dropped out to hitchhike around the country with my ex-husband. I have been painting every day and talking to God. I want you to know that I found myself again. I don't know how I lost myself so deeply in an unhealthy marriage and life, but I am now me again. The house on Sycamore represents the closing of a negative life and the end of bad choices I made, despite being a Christian. Now I'm living a life in God, and my husband is gone. I'm rebuilding my finances, but I'm genuinely happy. I have hope. Sorry for trying to use you, and thank you for being kind to me."

For me, it was a moment in time. This woman had gone on the much harder journey of spiritual connection to God on His terms. *She* had been the one to risk and follow Him. The word of knowledge about her street and the word of wisdom about what to do with her house had completely different purposes than what she had been pursuing me for, but God wanted her heart back. He wanted to help her be herself again. The risks both she and I took paid huge eternal dividends.

7

GOD'S SECRETS
REVEALED

O
ur Father's heart for us is to disclose His secrets. Let that sink in. The Creator of the universe, the sovereign Lord who says, "My ways are higher," wants to share His concealed mysteries.

I like how Webster's dictionary describes the word "secrets": "Kept from the knowledge of any but the initiated or privileged." We are the privileged ones. He desires for us to know His wonders. I don't know about you, but that blows my mind. If you're still trying to wrap your head around it (I wouldn't blame you), check out what Paul says:

What no eye has seen, nor ear heard, nor the heart of man imagined, what God has prepared for those who love him"—these things God has revealed to us through the Spirit. For the Spirit searches everything, even the depths of God ... No one comprehends the thoughts of God except the Spirit of God. Now that we received not the spirit of the world, but the Spirit who is from God, that we might understand the things freely given us by God. And we impart this in words not taught by human wisdom but taught by the Spirit, interpreting spiritual truths to those who are spiritual (1 Cor. 2:9-13).

Paul tells us that no one understands the thoughts of God except His Spirit and then in the same breath says we have received the "Spirit who is from God, that we might understand the things freely given us by God."

God wants to share His secrets with us. I love Proverbs 23:12, which says, "Apply your heart to instruction and your ears to words of knowledge."

Another of my favorite scriptures about words of knowledge is Colossians 2:3: "In Christ are hidden all the treasures of wisdom and knowledge."

The Greek word for "wisdom" here is *sophia*, which means having the knowledge to regulate one's relationship with God. This wisdom is associated with goodness. It also describes someone who is spiritually prudent with others and knows how to spiritually regulate circumstances—skillful, expert, sensible, judicious. Paul uses the same word in 1 Corinthians 12:8 for "word of wisdom."

The Greek word "knowledge" in Colossians is *gnosis*, which in this context means to know experientially. It is present and fragmentary knowledge, compared to the related word *epignosis*, which is used to describe more of a clear and exact knowledge, expressing a gained knowledge through education or participation. *Gnosis* is a present, intuitive knowledge. Again, this is the same word Paul uses in 1 Corinthians 12:8 for a prophetic "word of knowledge."

Words of knowledge help us to treasure who Jesus is and apply this nature to our everyday lives. It is a revelation in the moment of the knowledge that is in Christ.

Our Creator has absolute knowledge about everything, yet our human levels of knowledge are so limited. Paul says that we receive and impart God's knowledge—His secrets—not by human wisdom, but by the Spirit "interpreting spiritual truths." Words of knowledge help us to not only navigate through this complicated world but also to win in this world. Through this gift, God transmits His ideas and thoughts about something we have no ability to know—original thoughts that might even be completely unique or possibly a first for our society. Supernatural insight given directly to us by the Holy Spirit!

SEARCHING FOR HIS SECRETS

Throughout Scripture, we see the Holy Spirit referred to as the "witness." Romans 8:16 tells us that together with our spirit, the Holy Spirit bears witness that we are the children of God. This "inner witness" can also describe how we discern the thoughts and secrets of God from our own thoughts. As you grow closer to God, you'll learn the difference between His beautiful thoughts and your imagination. For some, this growth process can be annoying, painful, and frustrating. It can even cause people to give up.

I'm an extremely positive person who can find spiritual meaning in anything. I can watch a movie and interpret it into a spiritual parable, like Joseph interpreted dreams for Pharaoh. Granted, that doesn't mean my spiritual interpretation always comes from God, but my worldview and experience as someone who's on the lookout for God's secrets compels me to look for the spiritual meaning in just about everything I see. It's actually amazing to me that you can find so many expressions of God when you're being intentional about looking for them. Discovering the spiritual is just part of how I'm geared.

At times, this wiring has actually cost me when I've interpreted things through my own sensitivity and passion for discovering spiritual meaning. I've given advice or shared interpretation based on my own spiritual knowledge versus relying on God's knowledge or "witness" within me. When you spiritualize something, you don't get the same fruit that you do when you actually hear God's intention and receive a word of knowledge, with Him as the source. I love how Proverbs 23:12 reminds us: "Apply your heart to instruction and your ears to words of knowledge."

I've spent countless hours coaching people to decipher their complicated life journeys and pursuits. If I didn't apply my heart and my ears like Proverbs urges us to do and just left it up to life coaching or psychology, I would miss an ever-present God who desperately wants to share Himself and His secrets with humanity.

A few years ago, I was overseas ministering at an event in one of the largest churches in South Korea when a friend invited me to dinner with some elders of the church. These leaders had pooled their considerable resources to purchase the land for the church building and had paid for the construction of the church. They were not part of the event where I was ministering, but they wanted to meet us. I'm not sure they had ever been around a prophetic ministry like mine, but they were amazing God-hearing, God-fearing people.

The elders had heard that I sometimes did spiritual consulting work and asked what that entailed. I explained that it just helped people to discover their God-given identity for their project, company or campaign, and then to learn how to bridge their spiritual walk with Jesus with their occupation or vocation. One of the elders was intrigued and asked what that looked like. I explained that we could do a mini session together.

A few days later, I sat down with him and his family and asked him, "What is your business's spiritual calling?"

He didn't miss a beat and shared very matter-of-factly, yet still deeply: "I am to bring one million people to the Lord in my lifetime through funding the Kingdom. I have started several businesses and am using the revenue from them to create momentum for churches, media, and crusades."

"What is your greatest passion in this?" I asked.

"I love my children so much," he said. "I would hate it if they were dying and no one helped them! I want to help the children of this world connect to God!"

He was extremely passionate.

Then I asked, "What is your biggest roadblock right now?"

He explained that he was having issues with his partners that he had gone into business with but didn't mention anything specific. He seemed to be holding all of his cards tightly.

"What could bring a breakthrough with these partners?" I asked.

"Only a miracle," he said, looking defeated.

"Do you believe in miracles?" I asked.

"Yes ..." he said, sounding annoyed.

"Let's ask God what it will take to make that miracle happen."

We sat together for a while listening. He didn't really know why we were listening, but I was waiting for our friend and Witness, the Holy Spirit, to show us.

He didn't hear anything but I sure did! I heard the Holy Spirit whisper: *This man's partners brought false accusations against him in 2006, and his partners' greed has trapped them in a lawsuit together. They have frozen his assets and have paid bribes to some government officials. If he forgives them and commits to Me that he won't return to the easy route with shady partners who are quick to finance, I will resolve everything within a month.*

Then I heard: *The other party did everything they had accused the man of doing. To engage these lawsuits and trials any longer would take time away from him and his family.*

I even knew the type of business and some details that were core secrets to the case. I wanted to share these things with him.

I told him, "I'm having a spiritual moment. Do you mind if I share something with you that God just showed me?"

He smiled and clearly didn't know what to think about all of it, but he was open. I think he thought I was going to pray or something.

"Yes, of course." he replied. I shared with him everything God's Spirit had showed me. Instead of being relieved or happy, he stormed out of the room, angry. I looked at his wife, his adult kids, and our pastor friend who had brought me there. Everyone just ate in silence for a while. I didn't know what I should do. A while later, he came back.

"What you told me just now … no one knows," he said. "You either work for someone, you are a diviner, or you have heard from God. The details you gave me are all secret! If God is going to resolve these issues and vindicate me, it means I will inherit a lot of money again and that these men will go to jail. I don't know what to think. I don't want to forgive them, but I do agree that I made a huge mistake in partnering with them. I was just so desperate. I have committed to never again go into business with anyone like that!"

Then I looked at him and said, "If I was an investigator, I wouldn't be trying to lead you through forgiveness. If I was a diviner, I would want money and would not be using Scripture and connection to Jesus as my whole theological base. I'm just telling you what God showed me. Let's ask God one more thing."

"What?" he asked.

I prayed, "God, will You help me to forgive them as I choose to forgive them?"

He recited the prayer, and I could tell he barely meant it. But God took that "barely" and worked forgiveness into his heart.

"What if God wants to do something to turn this around?" I asked. "Is that what you want?"

"Of course it is," he said, "but it has been an eight-year legal battle, which has frozen most of our assets."

I shared with him what God had told me: "It will be done by next month."

I knew he didn't believe me, although he didn't say it. He didn't know what to think. He was definitely judgmental towards what I term spiritual consulting. We left and did our event at the church and went home. I can't say it was a happy evening or farewell. We just kind of left.

Fast-forward a month when I picked up the phone and heard the voice of this business elder.

"I can't believe it," he said. "My old partners were found to be corrupt in two other businesses they owned.

The newspapers even reported it, and one of the local headlines read, 'What Is Done in Secret Will Not Stay Secret.' And in the same article, my name was cleared. My whole company was turned back over to me, and they were completely shut down! I inherited all of their shares, double what I had! I can't believe that one night of prayer did this! It was exactly what you said!"

That day, he and I began an ongoing relationship that has been extremely fruitful.

HIS SECRETS BRING CULTURE TRANSFORMATION

Right when we were moving to Los Angeles to start our ministry and work here in 2006, a close prophetic friend prophesied to me about our future. He told me that I would "make history with God in historic buildings in L.A." At the time, I had no idea what that meant or would look like, but as I said earlier, I've learned to look for the spiritual.

As we began to scout for a building that would accommodate our ministry offices, a meeting space, and some sort of apartment or home to live in, I ran across a house rental online. It was a normal-looking Spanish house way above my price range and a little outdated inside, but I couldn't shake it. I felt like God told me to go look at it. As soon as I stepped onto the property, I knew deep inside my spirit that this was the house to live in for a period.

I told the friends who had come with me, "Something significant has taken place here for Hollywood. I wonder whose house this was?" I had a word of knowledge, a secret from God, that this building had been used for decision-making and mentoring for the entertainment industry. I felt the legacy on the property and that we were supposed to be there. I told all of our friends that this was the place. God had revealed a secret to me that would bring alignment with His purpose for us and our ministry.

As soon as we met the real estate agent, the first words out of her mouth were, "Hollywood history was made here."

Turns out the house was called "The Bennet House" named after a doctor-turned-film-producer. The whole street was named after him. He brought together groups of people with a passion for filmmaking and empowered them to take on projects they would have never pursued without the think tank groups. He was a mildly known historic figure, but what he did in that house in the Hollywood Hills was profound!

We rented the house at a reduced rate (that's a story for another time) and started our ministry there, in addition to hosting movie screenings, events, a few Hollywood prayer ministries, lots of parties, some film shoots, and more, all in sixteen months. It was so significant.

I love how a word of knowledge helped us to have faith for the house we needed, and God used my friend's prophecy and the house's history to speak to my team and me about our destiny in Hollywood. He boosted our faith and prepared us to plant a church later that year.

That word of knowledge helped bridge our faith to the work we were called to do and connected us to a resource that was way out of our league. Scripture abounds with this story in both the Old Testament and New Testament: Hearing God + receiving His revelation knowledge = a transformational impact for the world.

Back in Chapter 1, I talked about how God gave knowledge and wisdom to Daniel and his three friends so that they could advise the nation and help keep Israel safe. This is such a prototype for the days to come. God is giving Christians access to His knowledge and plans so that we can help bring His light to the world. When He downloads His knowledge and wisdom, our actions and words become relevant in so many diverse areas of society.

For decades, we have lived with this divine tension of the church separated from politics, entertainment, psychology, and so many other areas in our culture, and now I believe God is sending us out to influence these areas, which for so long we've had no traction or favor with through our own efforts. I can't tell you how many Christian therapists or scientists I've met over the past ten years who are literally getting revelation on how to bring ingenuity and wisdom to their field. In some traditions of Christianity, there's a school of thought that dualism (the belief that the universe exists separately from a moral God) doesn't allow our faith to affect these and other areas in our culture. But it's actually quite the opposite: Our faith proves that God is who He says He is in *every* arena of life.

God's knowledge and thoughts actually are transformative for the world around you. Think of the early church and how all of those business owners, government agents, Jewish scholars, and families gathered around the message of Jesus, sacrificing everything to see the gospel increase.

They weren't just hoping people would get saved and flee hell. They were confident of the promise of eternity and a King who would reign forever. They were living with a different mindset, which Jesus had modeled. The book of Acts is brilliant at showing some of the early leaders of our faith interacting in prisons, government buildings, businesses, schools, synagogues and homes to bring a clear message proclaiming Jesus as the one way to God. They demonstrated signs and wonders, which gave those around them the faith to believe their messages. They began to influence culture so fast that even death couldn't halt the gospel. In fact, news of martyred disciples and apostles only spread the message wider, deeper and faster. They weren't talking about a man-made institution; they were living and dying for a live gospel of God's unconditional love, which always has the power to create great change. Words of knowledge were always part of developing the wisdom of the early church leaders, and we see so many examples of that demonstrated in Acts alone.

I think of the apostle Paul and how in Acts 17 he received wisdom or a word of knowledge from heaven to know how to speak to the Athenians whose lives and public places were full of altars and statues built for pagan gods. Specifically, Paul spoke to them about their altar with the inscription "To an Unknown God." Through God's insight and knowledge, Paul shared a message with the inquisitive philosophers, leveraging their intrigue with the spiritual ("I see that in every way you are very religious," Acts 17:22) to tell them about the one true God, His nature and His desire for relationship with His creation. As a result of this spiritual knowledge describing the Athenians and their idols, Paul was invited back to speak and, more importantly, a number of people who had listened to him "became followers of Paul and believed."

Then there's the story I shared in Chapter 4 of Paul's vision of a Macedonian man who begs him to come to the country. Based on a revelation, word of knowledge or word of wisdom that Macedonia was ready for the gospel, Paul diverts his travel plans and, as a result, reaps a great harvest that brings regional transformation.

And it's difficult to talk about Paul's prophetic vision and words of knowledge for Athens without considering the secrets God revealed to Barnabus. He received a word of knowledge about Saul of Tarsus's conversion and leveraged his entire reputation in his community for a man known as a vile persecutor of Christians. This word (and Barnabus's obedience to it) caused such cultural transformation in the Roman Empire that just a few centuries later, Rome became a Christian nation, radically changing the spiritual landscape of the world from that point on.

God has an intention, and a will and desire for everyone and everything He created. I love that truth. So much of it is out of alignment right now, but Jesus paid a price so that one day everything will realign with God's original plan. We're called to see the world the way it's supposed to be and live with the divine tension of what it is now—standing in the gap for God's dream over humanity.

When we connect with the mind of God, He begins to show us secrets from those who are not in intimate fellowship with Him in the same way He gave Paul secrets about the Athenian philosophers. We begin to feel the pull of His divine will and exchange our thoughts and ideas for higher ones that come from Him.

Words of knowledge don't just lead us to prophecy for other people. They are also for our own individual lives, helping us to connect to God's current and original plan and to bring alignment to His masterful purposes and identity, or what I call our hardwiring. They strengthen our faith and restore our ability to fully walk toward His purpose, developing in us transformational thinking about the world around us. Having the mind and heart of Christ equips us to infuse spiritual meaning and knowledge into all sectors of life, assuring culture transformation.

HIS SECRETS SURFACE HIS INNERMOST DEPTHS

As I've said in previous chapters (but want to make sure you really get), words of knowledge are a means by which God gives us His favor, grace, increase, solutions, and upgrades. He speaks something to us that has a cause and effect.

Going back to the earlier theme of sharing headspace with Jesus, can you imagine how hungry people are to know what's going on in the minds of billionaires, presidents, celebrities, and powerful people? Researchers spend good money to learn what makes leaders like this tick: How did they become who they are? What was their process? What do they do daily that's different from what ordinary people do? Are there any patterns of life that we can replicate to be more successful or to have what they have? These are all common human thought patterns. Why do people idolize influencers? Because they're inspired by them.

Through words of knowledge, we actually hear the innermost thoughts of the most powerful person in the universe! We can discover what makes Him tick, what His dreams are, what He longs to do in the hearts of His creation. We can grow in our ability to carry His heart and thoughts in ways that make a difference to us and the world around us.

Think of it this way: I guarantee that if you married an investment banker, your finances would change. If you married a movie star, your social circle would transform. If you married a president, your authority would grow. In the same way, you have a God who covenants with you, and because of who *He* is, your opportunity and even identity will change and transform you.

The spirit of wisdom and revelation in Ephesians 1:17-23 is such a perfect picture of words of knowledge and revelatory gifts:

I keep asking that the God of our Lord Jesus Christ, the glorious Father, may give you the Spirit of wisdom and revelation, so that you may know him better. I pray that the eyes of your heart may be enlightened in order that you may know the hope to which he has called you, the riches of his glorious inheritance in his holy people, and his incomparably great power for us who believe.

That power is the same as the mighty strength he exerted when he raised Christ from the dead and seated him at his right hand in the heavenly realms, far above all rule and authority, power and dominion, and every name that is invoked, not only in the present age but also in the one to come. And God placed all things under his feet and appointed him to be head over everything for the church, which is his body, the fullness of him who fills everything in every way.

The Holy Spirit releases understanding to us so that we might really know Jesus the way He wants to be known. On top of that, the more we see Him, the more we understand His power and authority. He is the name above all names, the ruler over all authority. He has all power, not only now but forever. The closer you get to Him, the more you realize His authority. This has major ramifications for your life.

You just can't be friends with powerful people without their authority and confidence rubbing off on you. When we seek God's secrets through words of knowledge and pursue the depths of the heart and mind of Christ, we are in essence becoming one with God. His nature actually brings change and impact in us and through us.

I always think of one of the great men in Los Angeles whom I respect. He didn't have much of a childhood. When he got saved and began to really run after God, he had such a heart of compassion that he began a ministry for homeless teens. Because the cycle of raising donations to help with his work was so tedious, he asked God for two things: help with finances and help with his purpose.

Though he never really had a childhood and never really played with toys, this man began to have dreams about toys. Eventually, he paid close attention, as some of the dreams had actual plans and prototypes in them, almost as if he was an inventor dreaming of his next idea. One morning, after a particularly vivid dream, he drew the blueprints he saw in his dream, wrote down the plans, and then took them to a knowledgeable friend who was quickly impressed with what he showed him.

They decided to get the plans patented and were shocked when one of the largest toy manufacturers in the country licensed his patent. Money started coming in, but even better, this man started to have faith for more ideas.

He described the ideas as "downloaded from heaven." I believe if we search for and trust the scriptures that show us we have God's mind, we'll understand how He can drop complete thoughts into us—even whole inventions! We know many of the stories of American inventors, but if we dug a little deeper, I wonder how many of the great inventions we have today really originated with God—the original inventor and Master Creator—sharing His secrets?

HIS SECRETS SHOW US HIM

In His earthly lifetime, Jesus' example of what true a relationship looks like gives us a spectacular display of fellowshipping with the ideas of the Father in heaven. Jesus doesn't just hear His Father's plans. He also understands His Father's motives, intentions, and desires. He even starts to proclaim Himself as the representative of not only God, but says that when you see Him, you can see the Father in heaven (see John 14:9).

This is so amazing! Jesus is so in sync with God that He becomes a likeness of His Father's personhood.

To put it in terms you might better relate to, think about marriage and how the two become one through that union. If you've ever seen two happily married people after decades of marriage, they can fully represent each other. It doesn't matter if they're talking to a lawyer, a medical professional or a co-worker. They are so in sync with how their spouse would make decisions—what they would like, what they need, what questions they would ask—that they can advocate for each other.

When we hear words of knowledge (really, any revelation), part of it comes with who God is. We can dig into His secrets and see a mirror-like reflection of God.

HIS SECRETS SHOW US HIS PROMISES IN SCRIPTURE

One of my first times ministering at a church was in Australia. It was my first time being at the church. At my first session, I called out three to four names and dates, but they didn't match anyone there. I was new to this and started to feel my cheeks flush out of embarrassment, but I pressed through and we still had a good meeting. It just didn't involve a prophetic model or ministry. Thankfully, I had more sessions, which went fabulously after that first one!

About a year later after that meeting, Cherie and I had our second daughter, Hartley. About five weeks into her life, she contracted a very serious virus called RSV. I was scheduled to be at a church that I love and feel very close to, but because of Hartley's illness I was planning to cancel the trip so that I could stay home with my wife, my mother-in-law who was visiting, and our first child, Harper.

But Cherie really felt like I was supposed to go. She had been on staff at that particular church and felt totally supported at home. Hartley was looking better, though not out of the woods, and the pastor of the church called to say the church had been praying for healing and had sensed a breakthrough that the RSV was going to be better. Reluctantly, I went, feeling prompted to go but not wanting to choose this church experience over my family.

With so much going on at home, I hadn't had much time to prepare. I remember being in worship feeling very overwhelmed. I just couldn't pull my heart and mind together to speak. I had nothing in me to share. I cried out to God in worship and heard Him answer me but in a very unexpected way. He said, *Pull out the list from Australia that didn't work.*

Now let me frame this. I only had that list from one year earlier because I hadn't deleted my notes from my iPad. This particular list was a little sensitive for me because none of the words had worked out.

I thought to myself in a prayerful way, *"Are You telling me that those words I missed almost a year ago are for this conference? Those people might be here?"*

I pulled up the notes on my iPad and when it was time to take the platform I shared what had happened in Australia but told them I was going to try and use those same words of knowledge that night. People didn't know what to think. The first word was for a couple and I called them out by name and anniversary. Then I asked if they'd just had a grandson. They nodded. Then I asked if their grandson was named Greyson. They had tears and said yes.

"Hold it right here!" I said. "You mean the words that I had for you over your family, before your grandson was even conceived, have been in my iPad for almost a year? God really does know us before we were in our mother's womb. He knows our name before we are ever on the earth. He knows our frame before we ever existed anywhere except in His imagination! What an awesome God!"

I love how a word of knowledge experience can bring scriptural principles alive. It can make the God of the Bible who can seem far away to so many exist in the right here and now! It creates shock or awe in the person the words are about, but when you start to recognize these moments, you're changed by them too!

HIS SECRETS REVEAL HIS GREAT LOVE AND COMPASSION FOR US

I was at a church in northern California, called out a woman by name and asked if she had a boxer dog named Sydney that had passed away a couple of years before. She confirmed these words of knowledge.

I went on to tell her that her dog was with Jesus in heaven and that nothing we love gets lost (controversial I know—animals in heaven? Maybe I should write a whole book on that). Then I told her that her family was about to get a huge breakthrough, including her kids.

Well, that little word of affirmation was huge. Her family is a very strong leadership family in their church, and they had experienced a number of losses. She hadn't been in church for some time. In fact, when the boxer died, her youngest son didn't tell anyone about how angry he was at God and he went into a state of depression that had very quickly turned into a very serious state that required treatment. The dog was the last straw of a number of hard circumstances for him.

Then two years after the dog passed, I came through their town to the church she wasn't able to attend because of family drama and called her out! Jesus began to resolve the issue of the dog that started the spiral for her son. When she got home, her son had a very different picture of the God he was judging. God became a loving Father who was giving care to his dog until he saw him again.

Words of knowledge and any revelation we get from God help us relate to a Creator and Master who is so vast, so wonderful, so awesome, so deep, and so beyond us. Our human minds can only conjure up so much when we read Scripture. We need the Spirit of God to breathe life into us and to bridge us to this God who wants to be known by us.

Another time in my own church, one of our pastors who was speaking asked us to pray for the people around us and encourage them. I looked at one of the women in our church who I know but not very well (we have great friendship chemistry) and began to see a picture of a book called "The Book of John." At first, I thought it was literally the book of John from the Bible, but then I realized it was a man she was connected to and I saw the book shut. Then God set it up on a shelf and opened a new book and wrote a new man's name on the book. God was so compassionate looking. It's difficult to describe.

I told her what I saw, and she was shocked. John was her ex-husband whom she still had affection for; she had been hoping for restoration. She had come to resolve the situation with God but still felt shame from her divorce and as though her romantic life was somewhat over. Even though she had been to some counseling, she still felt unworthy.

She couldn't see God or His perspective over her romantic life. She could only see her past failure, which caused her to limit her self-worth and vision for what God wanted to do in her life. To bring the restoration He knows she needs, God showed His hand and heart to her.

I think of Jesus when He showed the Samaritan woman who He was in John 4. I know I mentioned this story earlier, but it was an impossible situation for her to see the Hebrew God. She was a Samaritan, which means she didn't know Jewish theology. Still, Jesus revealed Himself as the God of all creation—even of the Samaritans.

It is a wild, beautiful picture of His love that He gives us through revelation.

Hopefully, you're discovering that hearing words of knowledge is not just for personal ministry but also for a thriving life full of unexpected blessings.

The day before I met my closest friend, I had a dream about him. It wasn't a parabolic dream; I literally saw him. I felt like God was showing me friendship and I even heard His voice say to me, *If you sow into this guy, I will allow you to reap from his work because he will do greater things than you in his lifetime and in his family.*

I didn't totally know what that meant, but when I met him the next day, he was the exact person from the dream.

What I didn't know was that through this friendship I would learn so much about brotherhood, covenant, and loyalty. It has been one of my longest friendships to date. One word of knowledge to show me he existed changed both of our destinies forever.

So many times, we compartmentalize the use of a gift. But if we apply it to our relationship with God we can have faith in His ideas, thoughts, words—and best friends—which can reshape our lives and the world around us!

8

A GUIDE TO WORDS OF KNOWLEDGE IN SCRIPTURE

D o you realize that words of knowledge are one of the primary demonstrations of the voice of God? They are actually a main staple of how He spoke to His creation! Seeing all of the reasons God uses words of knowledge builds your faith in how He can use them in your life right now!

In the list below, I've identified thirty-three types of words of knowledge throughout the Bible. Our *Translating God Workbook* goes into more detail than these references, but I wanted to help set up your faith for some of the ways that words of knowledge can be useful.

I love the words of knowledge about transportation, finding missing people, provision, and identifying people. Seeing these examples in Scripture always helps me wrap my faith around this amazing gift. I pray the same for you as you take in the inspired Word. We hear God's thoughts and heart in ways that actually impact our lives and the world around us.

WORDS OF KNOWLEDGE IN THE BIBLE (ESV)

Identifying People by Name

Luke 19:5-6: *When Jesus reached the spot, he looked up and said to him, "Zacchaeus, come down immediately. I must stay at your house today." So he came down at once and welcomed him gladly.*

John 1:42: *And he brought him to Jesus. Jesus looked at him and said, "You are Simon son of John. You will be called Cephas" (which, when translated, is Peter).*

Acts 10:4-6: *Cornelius stared at him in fear. "What is it, Lord?" he asked. The angel answered, "Your prayers and gifts to the poor have come up as a memorial offering before God. Now send men to Joppa to bring back a man named Simon who is called Peter. He is staying with Simon the tanner, whose house is by the sea."*

Identifying Jesus in Situations

Matthew 16:16-17: *Simon Peter answered, "You are the Messiah, the Son of the living God." Jesus replied, "Blessed are you, Simon son of Jonah, for this was not revealed to you by flesh and blood, but by my Father in heaven."*

Luke 2: 36-38: *There was also a prophet, Anna, the daughter of Penuel, of the tribe of Asher. She was very old; she had lived with her husband seven years after her marriage, and then was a widow until she was eighty-four. She never left the temple but worshiped night and day, fasting and praying. Coming up to them at that very moment, she gave thanks to God and spoke about the child to all who were looking forward to the redemption of Jerusalem.*

Intimate Past Childhood Details

John 21:18: *Very truly I tell you, when you were younger you dressed yourself and went where you wanted; but when you are old you will stretch out your hands, and someone else will dress you and lead you where you do not want to go.*

Emotional Wellbeing of a Person

2 Kings 4:27: *When she reached the man of God at the mountain, she took hold of his feet. Gehazi came over to push her away, but the man of God said, "Leave her alone! She is in bitter distress, but the Lord has hidden it from me and has not told me why."*

God Appointing Someone to a Position

1 Samuel 16:3-5: *"Invite Jesse to the sacrifice, and I will show you what to do. You are to anoint for me the one I indicate." Samuel did what the Lord said. When he arrived at Bethlehem, the elders of the town trembled when they met him. They asked, "Do you come in peace?" Samuel replied, "Yes, in peace; I have come to sacrifice to the Lord. Consecrate yourselves and come to the sacrifice with me." Then he consecrated Jesse and his sons and invited them to the sacrifice.*

Acts 13:2: *While they were worshiping the Lord and fasting, the Holy Spirit said, "Set apart for me Barnabas and Saul for the work to which I have called them."*

Places to Stay/Eat

Mark 14:12-16: *On the first day of the Festival of Unleavened Bread, when it was customary to sacrifice the Passover lamb, Jesus' disciples asked him, "Where do you want us to go and make preparations for you to eat the Passover?" So he sent two of his disciples, telling them, "Go into the city, and a man carrying a jar of water will meet you. Follow him. Say to the owner of the house he enters, 'The Teacher asks: Where is my guest room, where I may eat the Passover with my disciples?' He will show you a large room upstairs, furnished and ready. Make preparations for us there." The disciples left, went into the city and found things just as Jesus had told them. So they prepared the Passover.*

Dream Interpretation

Daniel 2:18-19: *He urged them to plead for mercy from the God of heaven concerning this mystery, so that he and his friends might not be executed with the rest of the wise men of Babylon. During the night the mystery was revealed to Daniel in a vision. Then Daniel praised the God of heaven.*

Genesis 40:8-12: *Then Joseph said to them, "Do not interpretations belong to God? Tell me your dreams." So the chief cup bearer told Joseph his dream. He said to him, "In my dream I saw a vine in front of me, and on the vine were three branches. As soon as it budded, it blossomed, and its clusters ripened into grapes. Pharaoh's cup was in my hand, and I took the grapes, squeezed them into Pharaoh's cup and put the cup in his hand." "This is what it means," Joseph said to him.*

Personal Character

John 1:47: *When Jesus saw Nathanael approaching, he said of him, "Here truly is an Israelite in whom there is no deceit."*

Past Activities and Surroundings

John 1:48: *"How do you know me?" Nathanael asked. Jesus answered, "I saw you while you were still under the fig tree before Philip called you."*

Revealing Proper Identity/Hidden Motives

1 Kings 14:5-6: *But the Lord had told Ahijah, "Jeroboam's wife is coming to ask you about her son, for he is ill, and you are to give her such and such an answer. When she arrives, she will pretend to be someone else."*

Building Plans/Filling with Knowledge and Skill to Build

Genesis 6:14-22: *So make yourself an ark of cypress wood; make rooms in it and coat it with pitch inside and out. This is how you are to build it: The ark is to be three hundred cubits long, fifty cubits wide and thirty cubits high. Make a roof for it, leaving below the roof an opening one cubit high all around. Put a door in the side of the ark and make lower, middle and upper decks. I am going to bring floodwaters on the earth to destroy all life under the heavens, every creature that has the breath of life in it. Everything on earth will perish. But I will establish my covenant with you, and you will enter the ark—you and your sons and your wife and your sons' wives with you. You are to bring into the ark two of all living creatures, male and female, to keep them alive with you. Two of every kind of bird, of every kind of animal and of every kind of creature that moves along the ground will come to you to be kept alive. You are to take every kind of food that is to be eaten and store it away as food for you and for them." Noah did everything just as God commanded him.*

Exodus 35:30-35: *Then Moses said to the Israelites, "See, the Lord has chosen Bezalel son of Uri, the son of Hur, of the tribe of Judah, and he has filled him with the Spirit of God, with wisdom, with understanding, with knowledge and with all kinds of skills—to make artistic designs for work in gold, silver and bronze, to cut and set stones, to work in wood and to engage in all kinds of artistic crafts. And he has given both him and Oholiab son of Ahisamak, of the tribe of Dan, the ability to teach others. He has filled them with skill to do all kinds of work as engravers, designers, embroiderers in blue, purple and scarlet yarn and fine linen, and weavers—all of them skilled workers and designers.*

Identifying Pregnancy and Purpose

Matthew 1:20-21: *But after he had considered this, an angel of the Lord appeared to him in a dream and said, "Joseph son of David, do not be afraid to take Mary home as your wife, because what is conceived in her is from the Holy Spirit. She will give birth to a son, and you are to give him the name Jesus, because he will save his people from their sins."*

Luke 1:11-17: *Then an angel of the Lord appeared to him, standing at the right side of the altar of incense. When Zechariah saw him, he was startled and was gripped with fear. But the angel said to him: "Do not be afraid, Zechariah; your prayer has been heard. Your wife Elizabeth will bear you a son, and you are to call him John. He will be a joy and delight to you, and many will rejoice because of his birth, for he will be great in the sight of the Lord. He is never to take wine or other fermented drink, and he will be filled with the Holy Spirit even before he is born. He will bring back many of the people of Israel to the Lord their God. And he will go on before the Lord, in the spirit and power of Elijah, to turn the hearts of the parents to their children and the disobedient to the wisdom of the righteous—to make ready a people prepared for the Lord."*

Unveiling Sin

Joshua 7:10-11: *The Lord said to Joshua, "Stand up! What are you doing down on your face? Israel has sinned; they have violated my covenant, which I commanded them to keep. They have taken some of the devoted things; they have stolen, they have lied, they have put them with their own possessions."*

John 6:70-71: *Then Jesus replied, "Have I not chosen you, the Twelve? Yet one of you is a devil!" (He meant Judas, the son of Simon Iscariot, who, though one of the Twelve, was later to betray him.)*

Discovering Truth/Uncovering Lies

2 Kings 5:25-27: *When he went in and stood before his master, Elisha asked him, "Where have you been, Gehazi?"*

"Your servant didn't go anywhere," Gehazi answered. But Elisha said to him, "Was not my spirit with you when the man got down from his chariot to meet you? Is this the time to take money or to accept clothes—or olive groves and vineyards, or flocks and herds, or male and female slaves? Naaman's leprosy will cling to you and to your descendants forever." Then Gehazi went from Elisha's presence and his skin was leprous—it had become as white as snow.

Finding People/Lost Property

1 Sam. 9:19-20: *"I am the seer," Samuel replied. "Go up ahead of me to the high place, for today you are to eat with me, and in the morning I will send you on your way and will tell you all that is in your heart. As for the donkeys you lost three days ago, do not worry about them; they have been found. And to whom is all the desire of Israel turned, if not to you and your whole family line?"*

Recovering the Kidnapped

1 Samuel 10:22: *So they inquired further of the Lord, "Has the man come here yet?" And the Lord said, "Yes, he has hidden himself among the supplies."*

The State of the Seven Churches of Revelation

Revelation chapters 2-3

Directions/Assignment

Acts 9:11: *The Lord told him, "Go to the house of Judas on Straight Street and ask for a man from Tarsus named Saul, for he is praying. In a vision he has seen a man named Ananias come and place his hands on him to restore his sight."*

Acts 16:9-10: *During the night Paul had a vision of a man of Macedonia standing and begging him, "Come over to Macedonia and help us." After Paul had seen the vision, we got ready at once to leave for Macedonia, concluding that God had called us to preach the gospel to them.*

Healing

Acts 9:17-19: *Then Ananias went to the house and entered it. Placing his hands on Saul, he said, "Brother Saul, the Lord— Jesus, who appeared to you on the road as you were coming here— has sent me so that you may see again and be filled with the Holy Spirit." Immediately, something like scales fell from Saul's eyes, and he could see again. He got up and was baptized, and after taking some food, he regained his strength.*

Acts 14:8-10: *In Lystra there sat a man who was lame. He had been that way from birth and had never walked. He listened to Paul as he was speaking. Paul looked directly at him, saw that he had faith to be healed and called out, "Stand up on your feet!" At that, the man jumped up and began to walk.*

Resurrection

John 11:4: *When he heard this, Jesus said, "This sickness will not end in death. No, it is for God's glory so that God's Son may be glorified through it."*

Breakthrough in Circumstances

Acts 9:12: *In a vision he has seen a man named Ananias come and place his hands on him to restore his sight.*

Destiny

Acts 9:15-16: *But the Lord said to Ananias, "Go! This man is my chosen instrument to proclaim my name to the Gentiles and their kings and to the people of Israel. I will show him how much he must suffer for my name."*

Divine Connections

Acts 10:19-20: *While Peter was still thinking about the vision, the Spirit said to him, "Simon, three men are looking for you. So get up and go downstairs. Do not hesitate to go with them, for I have sent them."*

Knowing Others' Thoughts and Intentions

Matthew 9:4-8: *Knowing their thoughts, Jesus said, "Why do you entertain evil thoughts in your hearts? Which is easier: to say, 'Your sins are forgiven,' or to say, 'Get up and walk'? But I want you to know that the Son of Man has authority on earth to forgive sins." So he said to the paralyzed man, "Get up, take your mat and go home." Then the man got up and went home. When the crowd saw this, they were filled with awe; and they praised God, who had given such authority to man.*

1 Corinthians 14:24-25: *But if an unbeliever or an inquirer comes in while everyone is prophesying, they are convicted of sin and are brought under judgment by all, as the secrets of their hearts are laid bare. So they will fall down and worship God, exclaiming, "God is really among you!"*

Luke 5:22: *Jesus knew what they were thinking and asked, "Why are you thinking these things in your hearts?"*

Mark 2:8: *Immediately Jesus knew in his spirit that this was what they were thinking in their hearts, and he said to them, "Why are you thinking these things?"*

Matthew 22:18: *But Jesus, knowing their evil intent, said, "You hypocrites, why are you trying to trap me?"*

Warnings/Safety

Acts 27:10: *"Men, I can see that our voyage is going to be disastrous and bring great loss to ship and cargo, and to our own lives also."*

2 Kings 6:9: *The man of God sent word to the king of Israel: "Beware of passing that place, because the Arameans are going down there."*

Matthew 2:12 *And having been warned in a dream not to go back to Herod, they returned to their country by another route.*

Evangelism

John 4:17-26: *"I have no husband," she replied. Jesus said to her, "You are right when you say you have no husband. The fact is, you have had five husbands, and the man you now have is not your husband. What you have just said is quite true." "Sir," the woman said, "I can see that you are a prophet. Our ancestors worshiped on this mountain, but you Jews claim that the place where we must worship is in Jerusalem." "Woman," Jesus replied, "believe me, a time is coming when you will worship the Father neither on this mountain nor in Jerusalem. You Samaritans worship what you do not know; we worship what we do know, for salvation is from the Jews. Yet a time is coming and has now come when the true worshipers will worship the Father in the Spirit and in truth, for they are the kind of worshipers the Father seeks. God is spirit, and his worshipers must worship in the Spirit and in truth." The woman said, "I know that Messiah" (called Christ) "is coming. When he comes, he will explain everything to us." Then Jesus declared, "I, the one speaking to you—I am he."*

John 1:47-51: *When Jesus saw Nathanael approaching, he said of him, "Here truly is an Israelite in whom there is no deceit." "How do you know me?" Nathanael asked. Jesus answered, "I saw you while you were still under the fig tree before Philip called you." Then Nathanael declared, "Rabbi, you are the Son of God; you are the king of Israel." Jesus said, "You believe because I told you I saw you under the fig tree. You will see greater things than that." He then added, "Very truly I tell you, you will see 'heaven open, and the angels of God ascending and descending on' the Son of Man."*

Breaking Societal Restrictions

Acts 10:15–23: *The voice spoke to him a second time, "Do not call anything impure that God has made clean." This happened three times, and immediately the sheet was taken back to heaven. While Peter was wondering about the meaning of the vision, the men sent by Cornelius found out where Simon's house was and stopped at the gate. They called out, asking if Simon who was known as Peter was staying there. While Peter was still thinking about the vision, the Spirit said to him, "Simon, three men are looking for you. So get up and go downstairs. Do not hesitate to go with them, for I have sent them." Peter went down and said to the men, "I'm the one you're looking for. Why have you come?" The men replied, "We have come from Cornelius the centurion. He is a righteous and God-fearing man, who is respected by all the Jewish people. A holy angel told him to ask you to come to his house so that he could hear what you have to say." Then Peter invited the men into the house to be his guests.*

Provision

Matthew 17:27: *But so that we may not cause offense, go to the lake and throw out your line. Take the first fish you catch; open its mouth and you will find a four-drachma coin. Take it and give it to them for my tax and yours.*

Matthew 21: 2-3: *saying to them, "Go to the village ahead of you, and at once you will find a donkey tied there, with her colt by her. Untie them and bring them to me. If anyone says anything to you, say that the Lord needs them, and he will send them right away."*

Transportation

Acts 8:26-40: The Ethiopian's chariot ride

Luke 19:30-31: *Go to the village ahead of you, and as you enter it, you will find a colt tied there, which no one has ever ridden. Untie it and bring it here. If anyone asks you, "Why are you untying it?" say, "The Lord needs it."*

Passing of Dictator

Matthew 2:19-20: *After Herod died, an angel of the Lord appeared in a dream to Joseph in Egypt and said, "Get up, take the child and his mother and go to the land of Israel, for those who were trying to take the child's life are dead."*

Predicting Death

2 Peter 1:13-14: *I think it is right to refresh your memory as long as I live in the tent of this body, because I know that I will soon put it aside, as our Lord Jesus Christ has made clear to me.*

Choosing a Successor

1 Kings 19:15-16: *The Lord said to him, "Go back the way you came, and go to the Desert of Damascus. When you get there, anoint Hazael king over Aram. Also, anoint Jehu, son of Nimshi king over Israel, and anoint Elisha, son of Shaphat, from Abel Meholah to succeed you as prophet."*

Plans of the Enemy

Exodus 3

THE WORLD IS WAITING TO HEAR GOD'S THOUGHTS THROUGH YOUR WORDS OF KNOWLEDGE

Can you imagine how many big, eternity questions the world is pondering? Is the world going to get answers to these life-and-death questions? Are we?

God has wired us to thrive! When we're living a lesser life and need course correction. We have a natural, hardwired sensor in us that seeks God. His thoughts and revelations are major keys to accelerating humanity toward His heart. Just like when you're having problems in a relationship, you don't want to work it out by writing emails to each other or texts. It is just not as effective. If you can just FaceTime with the person or see them face-to-face, this can heal a multitude of fractures.

Words of knowledge help you rediscover life, intentionally place you in the center of your calling, and help give you a sense of direction and definition toward your purpose.

They also are one of God's main ways of protecting His promise and keeping the world on track toward the goal of Jesus getting to receive His full inheritance. So many people today seek out false spiritual advisors and consult the wrong people, in an attempt to get the right answers for everything from marriage and finances to direction and politics. It's time for Christians to grow in the revelation of God's heart and mind and become a source of His words.

YOU CAN GROW IN THE MIND AND HEART OF CHRIST

I want to encourage you that if you're fascinated by the prophetic, then be assured that God is creating hunger in you to reveal your passion. If you hear prophetic stories that invigorate you, know that you're supposed to produce your own prophetic stories. When I sat down to write this book, I wanted to ensure it would bring a perspective that would bridge you to helpful tools, to grow in these gifts.

We have a workbook and online course that can take you through practical steps in growing in words of knowledge, but I wanted to lay a foundation that might help you.

Like me and most others out there who are pursuing God, you'll have to work at connecting this way. As we've talked about throughout these pages, you'll have to practice and take risks. But at some point, rest assured knowing that God will share His mind and heart with you and will take the steering wheel. You'll be blown away by His presence through you and how He uses you to speak to others and to communicate His love for them.

Think about the ramifications of what I'm telling you—that with this one special gift, the Holy Spirit can help you share the same headspace as the mind of Christ and download what you could have never thought of on your own! Words of knowledge shouldn't surface in random, miraculous occurrences. Instead, I encourage you to focus on this as a lifestyle of pursuing oneness with God. This gift connects you to His thoughts and the innermost depths of who He is!

PURSUE OPENNESS IN YOUR HEART, SPIRIT, AND RELATIONSHIPS

I was ministering at an event, and at the end I took some time to model words of knowledge and prophecy. I am just so hungry to give people a glimpse of how I do it, in hopes that they'll catch onto it too. Most of the best things in life are caught more than taught, and I believe what

I'm doing now is baby steps compared to the quantum leaps God is bringing in the future! We can all do it.

At this particular event, a man came up to me. He was a local pastor and best friends with the pastor who had invited me. They had both started out very passionately, in a move of the Holy Spirit, but this was the first time in a decade that he had come back to more of a charismatic style of church.

"I can't decide if I think this prophetic thing is valuable enough to introduce to my church," he told me, "because in my experience people who pursue the prophetic and words of knowledge just create problems when it's overemphasized."

I could totally relate to what he was saying.

"I get it," I said. "It's not supposed to be our main focus, and many times people get wrapped up more in gifts than in relationship. That is, unless you set the appropriate goals and boundaries that allow this to be a relational tool. It seems like you've stripped the credibility of this gift set because of the imbalances you've seen it produce. Let me challenge you to do the work to set the boundaries and goals and see if you can re-empower the prophetic gifts to be a healthy motivator toward Jesus and relationships in your church."

He thought about that and realized that instead of doing some course correction from the pain he and others had experienced from these gifts, he had actually thrown them out. His version of being open to the prophetic gifts was, "Well, if God wants to bring these gifts, He will," versus *eagerly desiring* what God can do through them both in his life and others.

Anything you find great value in will require some work and effort. It starts with treasuring something and sometimes buying the whole field to get the one pearl of great price. If you've taken a hands-off approach to words of knowledge, I want to encourage you to pursue them! Take a season and see what happens when you apply yourself to hear God and get His thoughts.

I'm so grateful that God wouldn't let me give up on the prophetic ministry. It's one of the most beautiful parts of my life. I hope you also will pursue it because it will help you to connect to parts of God you would have never seen without these powerful gifts He has given us.

Now that you understand words of knowledge I want to challenge you to move into a place of faith. Your job is to keep your heart, spirit, and relationships as open to God as you can. We only have one lifetime, and we want to be as open as possible to let God work.

God has secrets that He has waited an eternity to share with you. Are you ready?

THE DIFFERENT WAYS
WE HEAR

We're going to walk through some of the many ways people hear from God so that you can identify, practice, or be aware of how God wants to talk to you. In our trainings, one of the most common questions people ask is, "Is it normal if I hear this way or that way?" Let me tell you there is no "normal" in God. There are no rules in how this all works; He is the God who calls Himself the creator. Can we really define an infinite God or put His process in a box?

I love how Jesus never did the same two miracles the same way. Thus, we have a God who doesn't give us scientific formulas for success in our relationship but rather tools to make it successful.

My wife was joking around with me one day and said, "You should write the book *Translating Women* as a follow-up to your *Translating God* book." I laughed and told her, "It would be a huge, thick book the size of a dictionary and would have nothing inside it except: 'I can't and you can't either, so don't try.'" She still thought it would be a bestseller.

God is more complicated than man's pursuit of understanding women, but just like men grow up and can't help but find great fulfillment in the opposite sex—through their mothers, their marriage and daughters—our relationship with God is so worth it!

God gave us so many tools for helping us connect to revelation. Some of you are new to the whole subject, so I want to define these tools to you. (Read more about them in our *Translating God Workbook* or other materials.)

TOOLS AND TYPES HELPING YOU UNDERSTAND HOW TO SEE

IMPRESSIONS

This is the number one way that I believe most people hear from God. I have gone over this throughout this whole book; it is the theme of having God download His thoughts or a picture into your mind.

> Mark 2:8: *Immediately Jesus, aware in His spirit that they were reasoning that way within themselves, said to them, "Why are you reasoning about these things in your hearts? Which is easier, to say to the paralytic, 'Your sins are forgiven'; or to say, 'Get up, and pick up your pallet and walk'? But so that you may know that the Son of Man has authority on earth to forgive sins"—He said to the paralytic, "I say to you, get up, pick up your pallet and go home." And he got up and immediately picked up the pallet and went out in the sight of everyone, so that they were all amazed and were glorifying God, saying, "We have never seen anything like this."*

Luke 24:45 *Then he opened their minds so they could understand the Scriptures.*

VISIONS

A vision is when you receive a word picture, a mental image, a daydream realm visual, a full moving picture, an open picture or an open visionary experience.

Acts 2:12: *"and he has seen in a vision a man named Ananias come in and lay his hands on him, so that he might regain his sight."*

Acts 16:9-10: *During the night Paul had a vision of a man of Macedonia standing and begging him, "Come over to Macedonia and help us." After Paul had seen the vision, we got ready at once to leave for Macedonia, concluding that God had called us to preach the gospel to them.*

DREAMS

Many of our dreams are sent by God through the Holy Spirit. At times, we can learn to interpret them; some dreams literally show us a future event or conversation in vivid color.

Job 33:15-15: *In a dream, a vision of the night, when deep sleep falls on men, while they slumber on their beds, Then he opens the ears of men...*

Genesis 37:5-11: the story of young Joseph interpreting his father's dreams that revealed future rule and his brother's future subservience to him.

TRANCE

A trance happens when you're at heightened spiritual awareness. You're more connected to God through the Spirit than you are to the world around you. It can be a dream-like state when you're awake.

> Acts 11:4-5: Peter began speaking and proceeded to explain to them in orderly sequence, *saying, "I was in the city of Joppa praying; and in a trance I saw a vision, an object coming down like a great sheet lowered by four corners from the sky; and it came right down to me."*

DIRECT VOICE

Sometimes God just speaks. It can be His audible voice, such as when someone else is talking and everyone can hear. It can also be a voice projected into your head that is beyond just thoughts or inspired ideas.

> Luke 9:35-36: *Then a voice came out of the cloud, saying, "This is My Son, My Chosen One; listen to Him!" And when the voice had spoken, Jesus was found alone. And they kept silent, and reported to no one in those days any of the things which they had seen.*

SMELLS

Sometimes God can use a smell or an aroma to be a word of knowledge. I remember smelling one of my best friend's colognes when I looked at a woman and asked if her name was the same as this friend. And it was.

FLASHBACK/DÉJÀ VU

Déjà vu is another spiritual language that describes an experience that much of humanity has had at one point or another—a feeling that you've been in the exact moment before. Sometimes, this creates an environment where you notice something you wouldn't have noticed if God hadn't made you present in this moment.

Psalm 77:11-12: *I shall remember the deeds of the LORD; Surely I will remember Your wonders of old. I will meditate on all Your work and muse on Your deeds* (NASB).

ABOUT THE AUTHOR

Shawn is an international speaker, TV host, spiritual adviser, producer, minister, and best-selling author of Translating God, among others. Well known for his strong prophetic gift and fresh biblical perspective, Shawn is passionate about seeing God's love, creativity, and justice ministered through God's people today. Shawn is also the founding pastor of Expression58 Church, a mission base and church focused on training and equipping Christians, encouraging the creative arts, and loving people in the entertainment industry and those in need. He lives in Los Angeles, California, with his lovely wife, Cherie, and wonderful daughters, Harper and Hartley.

G O D
S E C R E T S

W O R K B O O K

GOD'S SECRETS ARE READY TO BE REVEALED THROUGH YOU!

You've read Shawn Bolz's book *God Secrets: A Life Filled with Words of Knowledge*. Now boost your revelatory experience with this God Secrets workbook, a guide to activate your faith and teach you how to share words of knowledge in relatable ways.

God has countless thoughts toward you and those around you, and He reveals them through the gift of words of knowledge. Shawn's understanding of this gift helps make it easily accessible to you! Either individually or in a group, you'll grow in the following areas:

- Foundation – learn the history and benefits of giving words of knowledge.
- Intimacy – desire to know God's heart above all else.
- Identity – be real, be you.
- Accountability – grow in wisdom and humility with people you can trust.
- Risk – be brave, heal from any fear or need to perform.
- Hearing ability – so many ways to hear His voice; you cannot fail.
- Delivery – share from a heart of love in a relevant way.
- Faith – there's always room for more.

This biblically based workbook includes discussion questions and quizzes to help you get the most out of the practical wisdom and knowledge Shawn shares. Start activating your gift today!

And help fill this world with the knowledge of the glory of God.

G O D
S E C R E T S
a words of knowledge

e - C O U R S E

GOD WANTS TO GIVE YOU FULL ACCESS TO HIS SECRETS

Shawn Bolz has shared his book God Secrets with you. Now take his eCourse, designed to activate the gift of words of knowledge in your own life and release its power.

Join Shawn as he takes you through 5+ hours of teaching and activations to help bring you into a deeper understanding of words of knowledge and their application today. Either individually or in a group, grow in the following areas:

SESSION 1: **Foundation**
Learn the history and benefits giving words of knowledge.

SESSION 2: **Intimacy**
Desire to know God's heart above all else.

SESSION 3: **Identity**
Be real, be you.

SESSION 4: **Accountability**
Grow in wisdom and humility with people you can trust.

SESSION 5: **Risk**
Be brave, heal from fear or the need to perform.

SESSION 6: **Hearing Ability**
So many ways to hear His voice; you cannot fail.

SESSION 7: **Delivery**
Share from a heart of love in a relevant way.

SESSION 8: **Faith**
There's always room for more.

Get this biblically based eCourse to get the most out of Shawn Bolz's book God Secrets: A Life Filled with Words of Knowledge, and watch this gift fulfill your own life and that of everyone around you.

TRANSLATING GOD

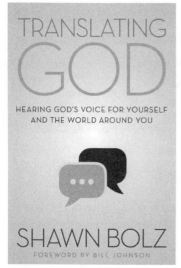

Through a thought-provoking prophetic ministry philosophy and Shawn's glorious successes and very real failures, you will be inspired and equipped to: learn how to hear God for yourself and others, grow through simple focused steps, take great risks, stay accountable, love people well, grow in intimacy with the Lord.

As an internationally known prophetic voice who has ministered to thousands from royalty to those on the streets Shawn shares everything he has learned about the prophetic in a way that is totally unique and refreshing. Shawn aims for the higher goal of loving people relationally, not just pursuing the gift or information, and he activates you to do the same.

Start to reshape the world around you with God's love today.

TRANSLATING GOD WORKBOOK

Be activated by Shawn's inspirational stories and use the activations, questions, and forms he includes in this life-altering workbook to chart your progress. Either individually or in a group, learn how to:

- Develope your relationship with God and others.
- Receive and understand revelation.
- Intentionally develop and nurture your prophetic ability.
- Become the fullness of God's expression of love through his revelation and voice.

www.BolzMinistries.com

TRANSLATING GOD STUDY COURSE

GOD IS SPEAKING EVERY DAY, AND YOU CAN BE HIS MOUTHPIECE.

Sometimes figuring out how to do that can feel overwhelming, but the prophetic can become a completely natural and love-filled part of your life.

You have the chance to help reveal the nature of God and show his heart of love through your prophetic gift. Hearing and sharing his voice is one of the most dynamic and exciting parts of Christianity, and it's actually one of the easiest gifts to pursue.

In this *Translating God* Study Course, Shawn gives you the practical tools you need to further develop your unique strengths and prophetic style. He also shares his insights, personal stories, and profound teaching perspectives to help you:

- Hear God clearly
- Apply God's love-filled revelation to your daily life and relationships
- Increase the depth and effectiveness of your prophetic gift

Translating God will change your perspective of the prophetic and bring depth to your revelation and prophetic voice. Shawn aims for the higher goal of loving people relationally, not just pursuing the gift or information, and he activates you through dynamic exercises that will help you practice doing the same. Great for individuals and group study!

This set includes:
- 9 video sessions on 3 DVDs (35-55 minutes each)
- *Translating God*: Paperback book
- *Translating God*: Workbook
- Poster: to advertise group studies

www.BolzMinistries.com

GROWING UP WITH GOD

Chapter Book

JOIN LUCAS AND MARIA AND FRIENDS
ON THEIR EVERYDAY ADVENTURES IN
FRIENDSHIP WITH GOD!

Lucas knows God talks to him, but he would have never imagined that he would hear such a specific thing about his year . . . and could Maria really have heard God about her destiny? They both have to wonder if God speaks to kids this way. Over the months that follow, God begins to connect them to other kids that grow into friends. Who could have guessed that by the end of the year, their lives would be so exciting!

Award-winning illustrator Lamont Hunt illustrates the rich, vibrant God journey of kids you can relate to. By best-selling author Shawn Bolz.

Workbook

An accompaniment for *Growing Up with God*, the children's chapter book, this workbook will encourage your kids to practice hearing God's voice.

Not only does this workbook teach children how to listen to God, it also gives them the tools they need to support and believe in themselves and each other.

In each section that relates to a chapter in *Growing Up with God*, your children will find:

- A reminder of what was in the chapter
- A true story from a kid their age about how he or she encountered God
- Three important things to know about God's voice
- Bible verses to back up the teaching
- Questions for them to think about and answer
- A prayer
- Illustrations from the book to keep the content focused & exciting

This generation of kids will be the most powerful, prophetic generation yet, and this workbook is a journal and guide will help them fulfill that destiny.

KEYS TO HEAVEN'S ECONOMY

So begins the unfolding of Shawn Bolz's visitations from God's heavenly messenger, His Minister of Finance.

Heavenly resources have only one purpose- that Jesus Christ would receive His full reward and inheritance in our age. Just as God held nothing back from Solomon, who longed to build a tabernacle for God on earth, God will hold nothing back from a generation of people who long to bring Jesus everything that belongs to Him!

God is about to release nances and resources to reshape the Body of Christ on the earth. God is looking for those who desire an open door experience with the One who is the Master of all keys, Jesus.

8 KEYS TO KINGDOM RESOURCES

Do you need Heaven's financial resources to see everything God has promised come to fruition? God created economics and resources to work best within the wisdom of his governing principles, and he will spare no expense at giving Jesus his reward through you. Us the foundational keys in this book to:

- Value love's expression through finance.
- Bring your life into alignment with Heaven's economic strategy and perspective.
- Gather the resources you need to ful ll your destiny.
- Further the kingdom and shape the world.

Finances and resources help us to father the world back into God's heart.
Let's do this already!

www.BolzMinistries.com